A LIFE IN  H

By Mil

BOOKS 1 and 2
1934 - 1946

PENARTH... Not the Centre of the Universe, BUT..."
Reminiscences of An Old Penarthian.

Book 1. **"Albert Road Boys First"**

Book 2. **"On the Home Front"**

Chwarae Teg Publications

Chwarae Teg Publications

An imprint of Chwarae Teg Publications,
7, Rectory Road Lane, Penarth, CF64 3AX.

www.chwaraetegbooks.com

ISBN: 978-0-9557340-0-7

Printed and bound in Great Britain by
Beacon Printers (Penarth) Ltd,
Leyshons Buildings, Cornerswell Road, Penarth, Vale of Glamorgan CF64 2XS

Acknowledgement is made to Dent (Publishers) for use of quotations
from "Under Milk Wood" by Dylan Thomas. (lines used in Foreword of
this book, but originally uttered by Rev. Eli Jenkins in his address to the
dawn from Dylan Thomas' play for voices, first broadcast on BBC
Radio.) Copyright permission granted by David Higham Associates.

"PENARTH......

Not the Centre of the Universe, BUT.............."

Reminiscences of An Old Penarthian.

ATTENDANCE

REGISTER

1. "Albert Road Boys First!"

Albert Road School,

Boys Department,

5 Class, _Fifth_ Standard,

Date when supplied to Teacher _1 SEPT_ 19**44**

_____ Director of Education.

Calendar Month ending 28th (29th)

31st MARCH, 19

Admission Number	Date of Birth D M Y	CLASS No	Name		This Quarter	Rule 18 CHART Etc.	Brought forward	TOTAL	1st Week ending 2nd Feb.	2nd Week ending 9th Feb.	3rd Week ending 16th Feb.	TOTAL	4th Week ending 23rd Mar.	5th Week ending 29th Mar.	TOTAL	Total
740	25 11 34	1	Adams	Peter	107		179	286							5	38 40 78
65	4 11 32	2	Spray	Peter	108		176	284							5	38 40 78
241	26 2 34	3	Clarke	Trevor	106		180	286							5	36 40 76
651	25 1 34	4	Ford	Michael	107		162	269							5	37 40 77
649	26 10 33	5	Frost	Peter	107		167	274							5	38 39 77
659	28 3 34	6	Jones	Stanley	107		182	289							5	37 40 77
647	3 4 33	7	Richards	John	96		157	253							3	35 34 69
420	30 7 31	8	Burton	Stanley	101		186	287							5	37 40 77
811	11 4 32	9	Laughly	Peter	106		184	290							5	38 40 78
551	10 8 31	10	Guy	Roy	97		138	235							5	37 32 69
442	29 5	11	Padworthy	Malcolm	104		136	240							5	38 36 74
650	7 10 33	12	Cullen	Arthur	103		75	178							5	37 36 73
896	28 9 32	13	Corbett	Leonard	108		186	294							5	38 40 78
649	3 10 32	14	Fairy	Sidney	108		186	294							5	38 40 78
668	30 1 31	15	Fleet	Oswald	78		186	264							5	38 40 78
567	7 4 32	16	Hansen	John	96		143	239							5	30 36 66
735	15 6 34	17	Harvey	Peter	107		181	288							5	38 39 77
556	30 8 32	18	Hunt	Kenneth	101		174	275							5	34 37 71
889	18 4 31	19	Hodge	Clark	106		180	286							5	38 38 76
891	19 6	20	Horton	Lionel	74		186	260							5	37 7 44
815	5 32	21	Kirk	Peter	108		186	294							5	38 40 78
774	5 2 31	22	Loftus	Fred	78		184	262							5	38 40 78
747	7 31	23	Kelly	Joseph	108		180	288							5	38 40 78
669	3 10 32	24	Mason	Stanley	104		186	290							5	34 40 74
571	14 11 32	25	Matthews	Howard	108		173	281							5	38 40 78
665	1 3 32	26	Phillips	Gordon	98		182	280							5	31 38 69
772	1 3 31	27	Morgan	John	78		184	262							5	38 40 78
711	1 6 31	28	Robinson	Cecil	88		186	274							5	38 40 78
816	6 32	29	Rees	James	106		186	292							5	38 34 72
734	10 7 32	30	Nixon	Stanley	108		186	294							5	38 40 78
650	12 32	31	Marshall	Howard	104		178	282							4	37 37 74
735	6 34	32	Major	Ronald	102		181	283							5	38 34 72
653	5 33	33	Culleman	Harry	107		183	290							5	38 39 77
420	32	34	Davies	John Ed.	108		186	294							5	38 40 78
432	32	35	Harlow	Frank	108		184	292							5	38 40 78
440	5 4 32	36	Morris	Fred	108		176	284							5	38 40 78
493	33	37	Blakey	Peter	108		178	286							5	38 40 78
757	5 32	38	Clark	Gordon	106		176	282							5	38 40 78
462	11 32	39	Smith	James	108		175	283							5	38 40 78
461	11 33	40	Shortland	James	108		186	294							5	38 40 78
724	24 5 35	41	Laws	Leonard	87		171	258							5	22 34 6
446	10 33	42	Lawson	Kenneth	84		132	216							2	35 39 6
734	6 5 34	43	John		104		162	266							5	38 36
924	14 11 34	44	Fricke	Colin	20			20								
1019	16 9 33	45	Minchem	John	20			20								
		46														
		47														
		48														
		49														
		50														
		51														
		52														
		53														
		54														
		55														
		56														
		57														
		58														
		59														
		60														

DAILY TOTALS	MORNING	No. Present	Early Mark	6038	39 39 39	40 40 40
		No. Withdrawn	Late	2	4	2 2
		No. of Attendances at Practical Instruction Centre, &c. Rule 12. Ad. Memo. 51.				
	AFTERNOON	No. Present	Early Mark	39 38	40 40 42 44	41 40 41 41
		No. Withdrawn	Late	2	2	2
		No. of Attendances at Practical Instruction Centre, &c. Rule 12. Ad. Memo. 51.				

WEEKLY TOTALS	TIMES OPEN		4	5	5 0 5 5	5 5 10 5 5	Times Open 20
	TOTAL ATTENDANCES (Including attendance under Rule 12. Ad. Memo. 51.)		159	159 411	411 413	421 411 209 209	1540
	No. ON REGISTER		43	43 43	43	43 43 43 43	Average 41
	No. of EXCLUSIONS (ART. 22)						

PENARTH.......
Not the Centre of the Universe,
BUT..............."

Reminiscences of An Old Penarthian.

1.
"Albert Road Boys First!"

By MIKE FORD

This book is dedicated to the Memory of

Peter Chick

Old Friend to all who knew him,
Man of the people,
Salt of the Earth,
Humorist,
Story-Teller

....

And, a very good Hairdresser, too!

FOREWORD

"PENARTH, NOT the centre of the Universe, BUT........"
Why the title? How did the idea germinate?

As, in my teens, I gazed out from the rear kitchen window at No 26, Pembroke Terrace (Now No. 12), and saw before me the vast panoramic bowl of Cardiff Bay, The Docks, The City, the hills of Leckwith and beyond to Whitchurch Hospital, Castell Coch, the distant wooded hills to Caerphilly Mountain and the entrance to the Valleys, and just below me, here on the hill topped by St Augustines'Church, known locally as "Top Church", the coal speckled grey mud flats and the wondrous ebb and flow, millennia old, of the tides of the Bristol Channel which twice daily covered and revealed them, covered and revealed them.....

I really DID think to myself, "PENARTH IS THE CENTRE OF THE UNIVERSE", My Universe....it had everything I wanted for a happy life, BUT.....

As time went by, but still at this same window with its panoramic view, I also idly wondered what lay beyond this "golden bowl".

Later I travelled far and wide and found out that "NO, Penarth is NOT the centre of the Universe, BUT, just like Dylan Thomas' Rev. Eli Jenkins of "Under Milk Wood": "I know there are Towns lovelier than ours, and fairer hills and loftier far, And groves more full of flowers......"

But just like him, now aged 73, I also begin tranquilly to ask:

> "But let me choose and oh! I should
> Love all my life and longer
> To stroll among our trees and stray
> In Goosegog Lane, on Donkey Down,
> And hear the Dewi sing all day,
> And never, never leave the town."

Home is where the heart is. Penarth is like a warm cosy winter coat or like one of its beloved old Street Chestnut Trees, offering warmth in Winter, Shade in Summer.

Wherever you may be, treasure your home and your memories of it.

Centre of the Universe, it may not be, BUT..............................

Mike Ford
Penarth February 2007

P.S. This is only a beginning. It is hoped to produce a whole series of collections of anecdotal and personally illustrated stories, following the life and times of "Little Mickey Ford", last of eight children to be born, at home, to William George and Mary Rebecca Ford at No. 26, Pembroke Terrace in the then County of Glamorganshire.

FOR MY GRANDCHILDREN:

ADAM, CERI, STEPHEN, RYAN, KATE, DEWI AND RHYS,

And ALL GRANDCHILDREN, EVERYWHERE,

To remind them that "Grandad" and "Grandma" have tales worth listening to.

Listen! And even record them, while you can!
If you don't, you'll regret it – always.

^^^

ACKNOWLEDGEMENTS   Thanks to:-

My Dear Parents,
   for giving me a secure and loving home and "quality" time aplenty;
Andrew, Cath and Seimon,
   for showing me "how".
Dr. Karen Mulcahy
   for her patient help;
Sue Hopkins, Elaine and Pauline,
   for encouragement in developing my meagre drawing skills;
Bob Cullen
   for enthusiastic support;
Ros and Emma of "Hi-Plan", Penarth
   for professional advice and speedy technical help;
Shira Valek, Editor: "Penarth Times",
   for giving me first opportunity of seeing my work in print
Penarth Readers of these anecdotes in our weekly "local rag"
   who have told me of their enjoyment.

And also to The Trustees of the Dylan Thomas Estate
   for kind permission to quote extracts from "Under Milkwood"

CHRONOLOGICAL SEQUENCE OF EVENTS (and sketched illustrations)

^^

N.B.   Dates given are only approximate, but memory is fickle.
The events are true, but the emotions evoked by these memories may have
coloured my descriptions and helped (or hindered) my later recollections.

Others, who shared these times, may have a quite different perspective.
If I offend, so be it......Mea Culpa ! Please Forgive ! (An Old, Old Man)

THE MAGIC OF CHRISTMAS
Albert Road Infants Department 1938

We are assembled in the Hall, singing carols by the Christmas Tree.

There is an excited mood of expectancy amongst us and amongst the teachers.

All at once we hear the sound of.... could it be? Yes, it certainly sounded like sleigh bells..... coming from the roof, high above us.

And now the large roof window opens and a rope ladder drops down as far as the floor in front of us.... an echoing cheer rises from us all as we recognize... Father Christmas, coming down the ladder, laden with a sack of toys! Our Teachers go forward, clapping, to meet him. And now the fun begins............

Little do we realize, in our innocence.... and innocence is universal and magical amongst children these days.... that the next-door Fire Brigade (Auxiliary Fire Service) has helped our welcome guest with his dramatic entry.

10

DOLLY MIXTURES... THE PRIDE,... AND THE FALL!

THE PRIDE

As a special (End of Term?) treat, our Class Teacher, Miss Edmunds has decided to buy some sweets, Dolly Mixtures, for the class.

But knowing that two of her charges, Shirley Delahaye and I both have relatives who own shops in the town, she must now choose which of us to patronise with her money.

Most of the other children favour choosing "Delahaye's" in Glebe Street as they know it as mainly a sweet shop, whereas my Aunts have a Grocery shop which sells sweets but not only.

Finally, I believe on the grounds that "Fords'" is just behind the school at the corner of King Street and Salop Place, Miss Edmunds chooses ME for the honour of taking her money and going to buy a large bag of Dolly Mixtures. Shirley cries but I am filled with pride !

THE FALL

Having taken the quick exit via the back wooden gates into Salop Place, I expect to return the same way with the Dolly Mixtures but find the gates closed and locked. And so I make my way back the long way via Coronation Terrace and down Albert Road, rushing so as not to be late back.

Suddenly I trip! New sandals and uneven paving stones! The bag has broken and the Dolly Mixtures are strewn all over the pavement and even into the gutter.

I carefully pick them all up, picking off and discarding all the grit and dirt I can see.

I get back, praying that no one will notice and that, once the sweets are eaten, none of my classmates dies !

Years later (decades, in fact), I own up to another of my classmates of that time ~now a lady in her fifties. To my relief, she bursts into laughter, not having realised that I had borne the guilt of this first unconfessed crime for so many years! BEWARE OF PRIDE!

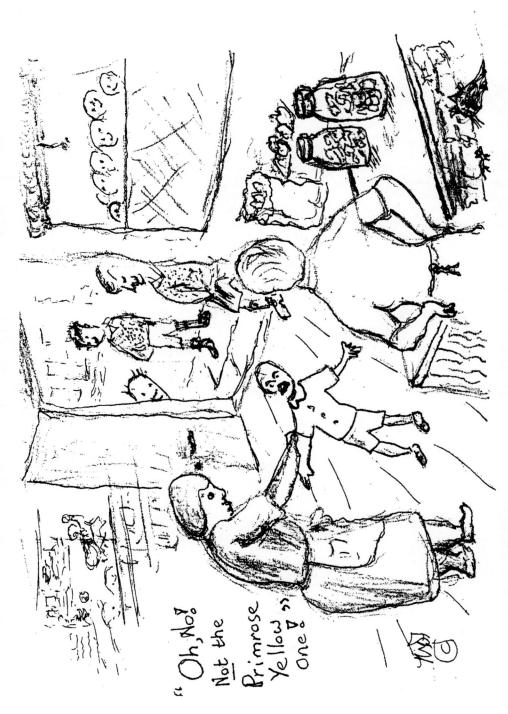

" Oh, No!
Not the
Primrose
Yellow
One "

"OH NO! NOT THE PRIMROSE YELLOW ONE!"

Living with the Aunts, at The Shop. Summer 1941

Perhaps it was because my eldest sister, Violet, had died of TB that the Aunts offered to have me come and live with them for a while so as to allow Mam to grieve. Both were childless although Aunt Alice was married to Uncle Joe but estranged from him. He also lived above the corner shop.

With such a seven year old child to look after, they indulged their fantasies of child-rearing, ignoring the roughness and toughness of Albert Road Elementary School, they had blouses made by a seamstress, BLOUSES ! ...whilst all boys usually wore the same cheap garments, almost a uniform, of itchy grey shirts, dark and often torn and sometime patched short trousers, long socks – usually "at half mast" and BOOTS.

Protesting at the Primrose Yellow ones, I would plead to be allowed to wear the Blue ones. Because they, at least, looked more like shirts ,,,although the rounded "Peter Pan" collars were a dead give-away !

There followed the expected days of torment at school and it was probably only an excuse on their part that the Aunts returned me home because I "had defied them" by going to see a film which they had forbidden. ("The Desert Song" at the Windsor Kinema)

Happily I went home to a "real Mam" who understood and made me a tough looking "Lumberjacket" and put me back into itchy shirts again,

THE VISITING STORY TELLER

ANNUAL VISIT OF THE PROFESSIONAL STORY TELLER

Those of us boys who had paid up the One (Old) Penny were duly assembled in the Upper Hall of Albert Road Elementary School – usually used as the classroom for Forms One and Two, the 12 –14 year olds. (Secondary Modern Schools not to be introduced until 1948).

This must have been about 1944 and an air of great excitement and anticipation was felt by everyone.
Of course our teachers would read stories to us, usually as a serial and I well remember the later popularity of Mr Roberts' Friday afternoon reading to us of "Midshipman Easy" by Captain Maryatt.

But a "PROFESSIONAL STORY TELLER"? Most of us did not know what to expect.

The "big boys" sat in their usual twin desks, pushed to the end of the hall, while we sat on the floor.

The Story Teller entered and in a most dramatic performance enthralled us. His facial expressions and wild movements held us and time sped by. So captivated were we that the watchful teachers had little cause to reprimand anyone.

I cannot clearly remember if the actor (for such he must have been) told more than the one story, but only much later did I realize that most of the performance was a retelling of "The Pied Piper". I am not even sure if our story-teller wore costume, but he certainly transported us all to Hamelin and his extravagant gestures evoke an image not only of a Pied Piper costume but of extraordinary, larger-than-life hands with which he mesmerized us.

"Flying
(at Penarth through
1944

FLYING
The day had started poorly. (Summer 1943 ?)

Every attempt to get my aeroplane off the ground from Pauline's next door garden had failed.

Admittedly, it was only two planks of wood nailed together crosswise, but surely as my brother George was already an RAF pilot it couldn't be that hard, I had even collected some big pieces of shrapnel from the gutters around Pembroke Terrace and had placed them carefully in an old OXO tin in front of me..

The Germans had dropped bombs over Penarth and Cardiff just a few days before and I wanted to drop their shrapnel back onto the Germans. But urge as I might, my aeroplane refused to move !

Anyway, George had promised to teach me to fly after the war.

Later in the day, The Triangle Gang had decided to relieve the boredom by collecting books "for the soldiers an' sailors an' airmen". We got an old potato sack from my Dad, "Pop" , my greengrocer father and started knocking on doors and asking for books. Most of the ladies in the town seemed pleased to hear our request and we quickly filled the sack. Then one of the boys suggested that, as the empty shop in the town, set up to gather books for "the soldiers, the sailors an' airmen", was probably already shut, we should just go up to Penarth Head and have a look at what sort of books we had collected. So sitting on the grass overlooking the cliffs and the sea, we examined our haul. After the first shout of "Bagseye !" from one lad, excited over some pictures, it became a scramble to claim the best books.

One large dusty old book fell apart and, from its loose pages, we started to make paper aeroplanes.

With the temptation of the sparkling sea spread out below us beneath the setting sun, we set to launching our 'planes into the air and very soon whole squadrons were soaring on the updraft.

"Now this is what I really call flying", someone yelled and happily we all agreed.

" No Smoke Without Fire "

"NO SMOKE WITHOUT FIRE"

St Augustine's Triangle – Probably Autumn 1943

St Augustines' Triangle (also known locally as "The Plantation"), a piece of sloping grassy wilderness, punctuated by shrubs and trees and bordered at that time along the top road, Church Place North, by old railings opposite the walls of St Augustines' churchyard, was for us children: "OURS"...a place to meet, climb trees and tear the seats out of our pants, fall from breaking swing ropes while being "Tarzan", light fires and cook spuds and sometimes camp out directly under any old piece of canvas we could find and creep the few yards surreptitiously home in the night if wet, cold or just "homesick"!

One day I set out to call on my bosom pal Arthur, who lived just around the corner, down the hill and just opposite the bottom end of The Triangle. I meant to cook a few spuds with him, so I took the box of matches from the side of the gas cooker and set off.

To save time, I pushed a few scraps of paper under the railings at the top of "The Plantation", lit them and ran off to fetch Arthur, thinking to myself: "That'll save time...nice fire all ready for us !".

Arthur was out. No-one at home. I may have looked for him at the far end of The Triangle, but only vaguely heard a sound of strange roaring and also that of a bell clanging insistently from afar.

Wandering back, with a great shock I saw the Firemen now tackling a huge blaze threatening to engulf the corner of The Plantation, which I had left only, it seemed, minutes before. Running up, I tried to help by beating out the smaller flames nearest to me with a piece of orange-box rope I had meant to make a swing out of.

Quelling the fire, the firemen turned to me smiling and thanked me for my help. Proudly, the hero of the hour, I bashfully basked in all the glory.

The whole effect was ruined however when Mam appeared. She had missed the box of matches, heard and seen the fire and guessed who the culprit had probably been ! Shamefacedly, I had to own up and listen to a lecture from the now angry firemen.

NEVER, NEVER, EVER, PLAY WITH FIRE!

"Curiosity and the coconut."
(———'s class – 1943)

CURIOSITY AND THE COCONUT

It is 1944 and I am in Mr Smith's Class. He is quite a friendly teacher but the classroom is uninspiring.

The usual class-work is repetitive and follows quite strictly a "3 Rs" programme. Reading, (W)riting and (A)rithmetic comprising Mental Arithmetic, Four Rules of Number, Times Table chanting, Spelling, Handwriting and Composition. Occasionally we are treated to "Physical Jerks" in the outside, high-walled enclosed top yard of Albert Road Elementary School. We are in Standard 4 and are being prepared methodically for the following year's Scholarship Examination from which just five of us will emerge successfully and transfer to The County Grammar School for Boys. (as against Victoria School's 20 +.) Those less fortunate will remain for a further two years and will leave school at 14 to start work. But they will have woodwork lessons in the adjoining end-of-terrace house and their other lessons in the top hall, taught by the Headmaster, Mr Williams.

Mr Smith may once have told us the history of the coconut, now gathering dust perched atop the tall cupboard behind his teacher's desk. Now, whilst everyone else, heads down, is working on his set of multiplication sums, I gaze at the coconut and wonder….."Where from? What's it like there?" It is still wartime and fresh coconuts are a rarity, never seen nowadays in the shops. I daydream on and on, only to awake with a start to find blood trickling down my forehead. I had fallen asleep and in falling, had caught my head on the edge of my desk, leaving a slight dent in the middle of the forehead. This still reminds me, even today – almost sixty five years later – of that scene and that darned coconut!

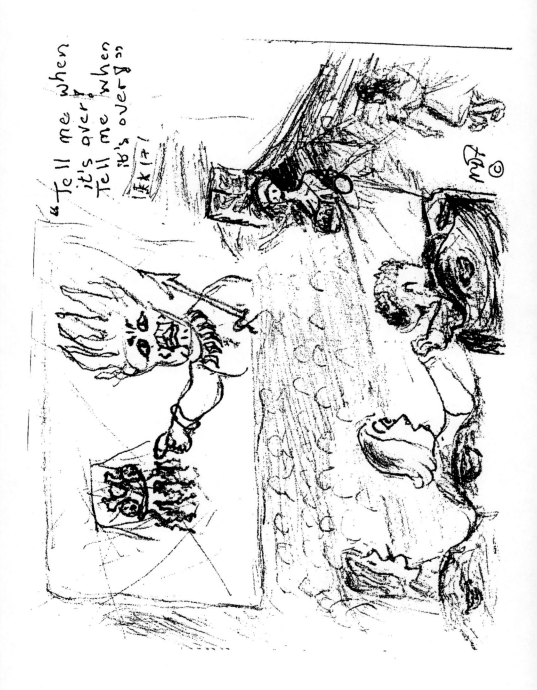

"TELL ME WHEN IT'S OVER, TELL ME WHEN IT'S OVER!!!"

Washington Cinema – Sometime 1943 – 44

During the War Years (1939 – 1945) cinema-going was at its height. Penarth boasted two cinemas: "The Washington" (known amongst the cognoscenti as "The Washhouse") and the "Windsor Kinema" (a.k.a. "The Fleapit). With three changes of programme at each, it was possible, if you could get in – such were the long queues – to see six different programmes each week, visiting daily, Monday to Saturday. The almost three-hour-long programmes of main feature, B film, News, etc were shown continuously from just after midday until about 10.30 p.m. and, if you could dodge the usherette's torchlight beam searching for miscreant children, you could stay there for hours on end. Saturday matinees for kids ended with all emerging sometimes blinded by bright sunshine like troglodytes from some black cave and passers-by could always tell from their antics what the kids had seen.... shadow sword fencing and being "Zorro" or thigh slapping and whooping as only real "Windybums" could, firing imaginary arrows, as they stumbled in hordes down the steps of the Washhouse.

My bosom pal at this time, Arthur and I went nearly everywhere together and often to the cinema. He was always a great help to me. Of ever nervous disposition, I relied on him to help me avoid seeing any "scary" part of a film, and although quite tame compared to modern horror films, for me unbearable. I would bury my head in my lap, close my eyes and grasp his hand urgently* and beg him to "tell me when it's over, tell me when it's over!"

On one occasion, forgetting that Arthur had not come that time and nervously anticipating a particularly gory scene, I grabbed the hand of my immediate next-seat neighbour but not hearing the usual confirmatory grunt from Arthur to my repeated plea, I looked up to find myself clutching the hand of a startled little girl! With great embarrassment at the accusing stares from all around, I quickly left.

* N.B. To cynics who leer knowingly, "Oh Yeah! nudge, nudge, wink, wink" I plead innocence/nerves!

Top Row: From the Ford Family Album (From Left to Right)
Brothers. Jack and George; Sister Violet, Mam, Sister Bea;
Author (6 yrs); Sister Enid and Author (age 12)

Middle Left: Pembroke Terrace: No 26 is second from Right.

Bottom Row: Stanwell Crescent (Scene of "A Spring Offensive")
Present Day Albert Primary School (former "Elementary School")

LAST BANANA BOAT IN PENARTH

"LAST BANANA BOAT IN PENARTH"
E.W.S. Reservoir (Emergency Water Supply) – St Augustine's Road

Although Penarth is by the sea, access to it for boating seemed impossible and just about only for the privileged. The Docks Motor Boat, Fishing and Sailing Club had either yet to happen or was unknown to us.

One of the Gang, probably Malcolm C., had the bright idea of building a boat and sailing it on the E.W.S. tank just opposite The Triangle in the lower field. As to materials, well obviously a Fyffes' Banana box could form the hull and its removed heavy wooden hinged lid, sawn in half, could provide the sharp end. Getting a box from my father's store was easy enough and with our crude attempts at carpentry, we quickly nailed on the prow. Now we were ready for the launch and maiden voyage of our good ship, HMS Banana.

The water of the E.W.S. tank was murky, to say the least. Dead cats, amongst other objects had found their last resting place here. Scarcely had we launched our vessel than we started to take in water.

Fortunately for us, some adult had seen our activities and had quickly rung the Fire Service. Almost immediately an A.F.S. van pulled up with a screech and two fire officers emerged, shouting. The other lads scarpered. We slowly and ignominiously paddled to the waiting fireman. We were warned and our confiscated boat taken away in the van.

Badly shaken by our experience, we realized how easily our Good Ship Banana might have become a Yellow Submarine and we resigned ourselves to a healthier "landlubber" life!

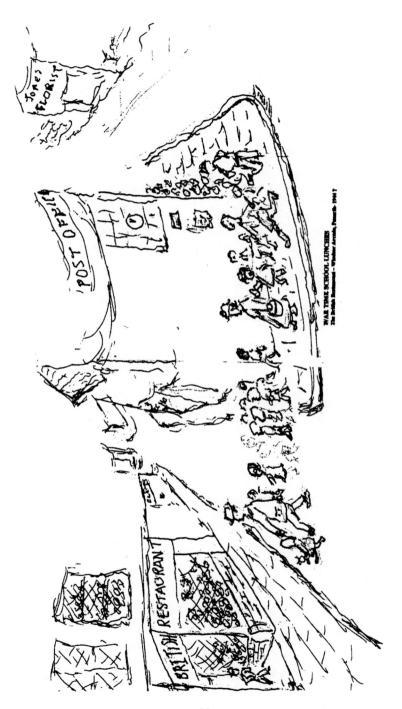

WAR TIME SCHOOL LUNCHES
The British Restaurant – Walthew Arcade, Pemaen 1941 ?

WAR TIME SCHOOL LUNCHES
The British Restaurant - Windsor Arcade, Penarth, 1944.

In order that everyone in Britain during the War should be able to get a hot economic meal, made from available healthy ingredients, a chain of "British Restaurants" was established throughout the land.

These were usually used by travellers away from home and did not require any food coupons.

Penarth's British Restaurant was located in the shop at the right hand side, Ludlow Lane end, of the Windsor Arcade. For a short period, we - the pupils of Albert Road Elementary School – were marched down to have our daily lunch there.

Later, perhaps just after the war, our school meals were prepared and served in the Old St Augustine's Institute in Albert Road.

"ALBERT ROAD BOYS FIRST XI"

HAIRCUTS

1942 – 46   Mr Baker's at Corner Shop, Glebe Street/Salop Street
1960 -   Peter Chick's, Glebe Street (just a few doors from the old Corner Shop)

Mr BAKER'S....and nearly all Gents' Barbers of the day, gave "no nonsense" haircuts and, for boys, plain "Old Pudding Bowl" was the only "style", with a straight fringe cut across the forehead.

It was painful too! Just beside the one and only barber's chair was a small white sterilizing cabinet with three serried glass doors. From this came strong chemical fumes which, not only most effectively killed off any wildlife present on combs and brushes placed within, but also stung the eyes of " 'im in the chair".

Other waiting boys were always watchful of the current victim to see if he "blubbed" and could be taunted with the cry of "Cissy! Cissy!"

To my later shame but then innocence, I followed Mr Baker's instruction that I must turn my head slightly to the left and downward and look at the cardboard cut-out advertisement below the shelf in front of me. It depicted a young woman, in one-piece bathing costume poised ready to dive into a cave-grotto pool. He assured me that if I watched the lady carefully the lady "will dive into the pool any minute now!" I waited in vain, but for several years afterwards I always watched and waited! Such faith and such innocence in a world of adults!

PETER CHICK'S. Now, years later, I regularly visited Peter's shop. Although the seating was old and worn and the shop always crowded, the welcome was always warm and Peter's shout of "ALBERT ROAD BOYS FIRST!", equally homely and jolly.

Now a teacher myself at Albert Road Junior School, we shared the same memories and tales. I suspected that some of my fellow unshorn were former classmates of mine, but couldn't always be sure.

One day a strong burning tickle in my nose alerted me to a familiar presence. NO! I couldn't believe it!

YES – there stood the old sterilizing cabinet which Peter evidently had rescued from the old shop!

Leaving his barbers' shop that day, I was proud that at least I hadn't "blubbed".... or more importantly been seen to do so.... even though, if I'm honest, my eyes were just a bit moist!

PLAYTIME
(or War-Zone?)
Winter 1944

PLAYTIME?

(or "War Zone"?) Winter 1944

GAMES? Apart from a few football enthusiasts, using discarded coats for goals, the traditional Sports(?) for the older boys, anyway, seemed to be either "Strong Horses" which according to elder brother Jack (16 years my senior) had been played for generations and "BLACK HOLE" – of Calcutta, presumably. For the latter, a temporary corrugated iron shed with two open doorways was used. This must have been the protective shelter, against flying shrapnel, for night-patrolling air-raid wardens. Its daytime and therefore more entertaining use was for the older, bigger boys to experiment with its physical properties, i.e. to find out how many smaller boys they could catch and crush into "The Black Hole".

STRONG HORSES. This ancient sport was more like a rugby scrum in which opposing teams tried to construct from their own bodies a sort of bridge or "strong horse" onto which their opponents would fling themselves and try to break its back.

TEACHER ON DUTY. This is the gentleman in an overcoat and smoking a pipe.

He is in the playground only to make sure that no child actually dies, while he is "On Duty" and to take a ten-minute smoking break. If a boy breaks a leg or worse, he will offer the prompt advice to: "Go and have a drink of cold water and then rub it better !"

BOOTS. No self-respecting Albert Road Boy would ever wear shoes. Shoes are only for "cissies" and even though boots may be worn down at heel, broken or torn, that just shows how tough and rough Albert Road Boys are, from the rougher, tougher end of town !

Disaster in Panjo Jones Year 44
The Potato Avalanche

26.2.07

DISASTER IN "PANCHO" ROBERTS' CLASS
The Potato Avalanche

It is 1945 and I am in "Pancho" Roberts' Class. It is the "Scholarship" class and half-a-dozen of us are given extra coaching by the Headmaster, Mr Williams. Perhaps on this day, in addition to the "3Rs", we are practising one of the "compositions" to be expected in the Scholarship Exam., passing which would allow those successful to go on to the Grammar School and maybe, much later, to College. Those who "failed" this "11 plus exam", would have to stay on for two years in Albert Road Elementary School, leave school and start work at 14 years of age.

Probably, the topic of today's composition would be an old favourite, "The Autobiography of a Shilling" and having gone over all the possible adventures of this coin during its lifetime, Pancho is writing a few helpful words and phrases on the blackboard.

As is also usual amongst our teachers, trying to help tradesmen and their families in this poorer area of the town, Pancho has asked me to bring him some potatoes from my greengrocer father.

Suddenly, on the shelf beneath my desk, the paper bag splits open and the potatoes cascade onto the floor and noisily bounce down from level to level in our tiered classroom. I am mortified but the rumpus causes great hilarity amongst my forty or so classmates. "Pancho" is kindness itself but it takes him a considerable time to restore some kind of order amongst my boisterous classmates and for the composition lesson to continue!

SOUP ANYONE?

Pembroke Terrace – next to Sea Cadet Hut – Autumn 1944

My Aunts at the corner shop behind Albert Road School were very good cooks, particularly Aunt Grace.

Times were hard and perhaps just to help out, occasionally I was called on to carry home a jug of Aunt's hot soup to Pembroke Terrace – only a few streets away.

Once, approaching home carefully carrying the hot jug of steaming soup, around the corner ahead came roaring down on me two class-mates, Stan and Nobby. Always of a nervous disposition and fearing any blows to come, I used the only weapon, literally, to hand: the soup. I flung the hot and sticky contents of the jug all over them!

They stopped as though shell-shocked.

Then they hit me anyway and ran off homewards.

I stood there crying, but still stooping to pick up and hurl after them all the soup's solid ingredients which lay in the gutter.... carrots, dumplings, potatoes and other assorted vegetables.

Now came a greater worry. How would I explain to Mam and my hungry sisters what had become of the soup. I needn't have worried. Everyone burst into laughter at the thought of how Stan and Nobby would explain to their mothers how they had come to arrive home, plastered in soup!

"TOWN BOY ...OR HOME BOY?"

"TOWN BOY OR HOME BOY?"

This was the question of late-arrivals who had to enter the boys' department via the top hall, where the Headmaster presided over forms One and Two. The "big boys" looked on as the defaulters queued up miserably to be quizzed. It must have been a most interesting daily spectacle for them, but they tried to hide their glee or mirth at the innocent and guileless responses of the younger boys or wince at the savage punishment meted out to those answering this seemingly innocuous question incorrectly. They, heads down, would always pretend to be totally absorbed in their set work, only daring to guffaw if a particularly naïve reply brought a smile or chuckle to the Headmaster's face. But this only happened rarely.

And so the Inquisition would begin:
"TOWN BOY OR HOME BOY?"
"Town boy, Sir!"
"ALRIGHT DON'T BE LATE AGAIN! WHY WERE YOU LATE, ANYWAY?"
"Mam couldn't find me socks, Sir." (A smile, maybe a chuckle with half-stifled sniggers as a chorus) (gruffly but with a half-smile) ALRIGHT, ALRIGHT, OFF TO YOUR CLASS!...... NEXT!!!"
"Next" gives the wrong reply, " Home Boy, Sir."
"UP TO NO GOOD, I'LL BE BOUND! RIGHT, HOLD OUT YOUR HAND!"

The cane swishes ending with a loud CRACK! The Home Boy nurses his now stinging hand and retreats to his classroom. The "big boys" bend more earnestly over their desks and the school day continues.

"Home Boys" came from the "Gibbs' Home", an orphanage or centre for wayward children, founded by local Methodist philanthropists and later to become "Headlands Residential School" run by National Children's Homes. Now it has its own school within its own grounds but at that period boys were marched to Albert Road Elementary School in a crocodile and any "Home Boy" arriving late was deemed to have dodged the column and been "up to no good". Therefore in those harsh days this was considered just punishment and quite normal. But poor kids – double jeopardy – to be an orphan AND punished for it, too !

VICTORY IN SIGHT – A SPRING OFFENSIVE

Battle of "The Mornners and The Jonners" - the fight for Stanwell Crescent Hill
Spring 1945

The adjoining streets of John Street and Maugham Street (our street "argot" had us pronounce it "MaughAN Street just as "chimneys" was always pronounced, "chimLEYS") produced two nebulous gangs, called respectively, "The Mornners" and "The Jonners". No formal application for membership was necessary and this certainly wasn't exclusive. You could come from anywhere in the North end of town and no barriers arose from age, gender or ethnicity! Quite Democratic, really. We only came together, spontaneously it seemed, when the mood just happened. Leaders then emerged from amongst the older lads, probably still at Albert Road Elementary School and therefore probably thirteen or fourteen years old.

Besides occasional air-raids, the blackout and rationing to remind us that Britain (and Penarth) was still at war, most of us had relatives in the Armed Forces, so together with the older folk left at home we listened to the "wireless" (radio) and kept up with the war news. Some of us even had large world maps pinned up at home, where advances and victories were "flagged" (marked out). So we couldn't help but be aware of "the final push", and kids, being kids, we had to imitate – hence this Street Battle. Neither side was identified as "Allies" or "Axis". We just re-enacted what was going on in the wider world which awaited us.

Begging, borrowing or by other means, many of us managed to "acquire" tin helmets and The Mornners and The Jonners assembled, we at the top of the hill, the "enemy" at the bottom. We never did discover how this was wangled but some current Field Marshal must have learnt his tactics, if not from the Playing Fields of Eton, then from such juvenile street skirmishes such as ours!

Armed with stones and half-bricks, we attacked with as fierce roars as we could yell although, probably, our leaders, with adolescent voices painfully breaking, kept quiet. A hail of badly aimed missiles roused the local housewives and they appeared, most intimidatingly rebuking individuals by name and warning of CONSEQUENCES! Sheepishly, as of one accord, we abandoned the valiant battle and crept off! But, only momentarily rebuffed as each side, now back in their own native areas, claimed the Victory and proudly marched through the streets, loudly chanting: "WE WON THE WAR! WE WON THE WAR!"

As far as I know there had been no casualties, no windows broken – but nevertheless:

IT HAD BEEN A FAMOUS VICTORY !

"PEACE and ICECREAM"

FORTES

42

PEACE AND ICE CREAM
Penarth Esplanade – Summer 1945

Peace had arrived at last and to help the nation celebrate, restrictions were lifted on the public sale of Ice Cream and confectionery. For the whole six years of war, a weekly ration of sweets had been only two ounces per person or the equivalent of one small bar of chocolate per week. This new freedom had been announced over the wireless and "Fortes", the pre-war ice-cream parlour "on the front" was to open early on the morrow........ Quickly a group of Mams from the Docks area decided that we would have our own Victory Parade down to Fortes to have our first Peacetime Taste of Ice Cream. Everyone should dress up in costume. Wardrobes were raided, old jewellery boxes emptied and big brass curtain rings purloined – for the pirates' earrings, of course. Corks were burnt and faces daubed. Eye patches were treasured. Even Long John Silver himself would have been proud of us!

The morning came and a motley crew assembled and marched proudly down Beach Hill towards Fortes – resplendent, if I remember correctly, with a gaily striped awning. Inside, reminiscent of pre-war days, unaccustomed and seemingly long unvisited cane armchairs and glass-topped cane tables awaited us.

My pride quickly evaporated as I overheard the frosty and contemptuous remarks of a by-standing, very erect and well-dressed couple, "Disgusting!" Suddenly I saw US "as others see us": as "a raggle-taggle band of gypsies, oh!". Miserably, Penarth's Old Guard of the still surviving Class System had struck again.

But after one, two, or maybe even three of Fortes' "Knick-a-Bocker Glories", Heaven seemed to shine down on us again!

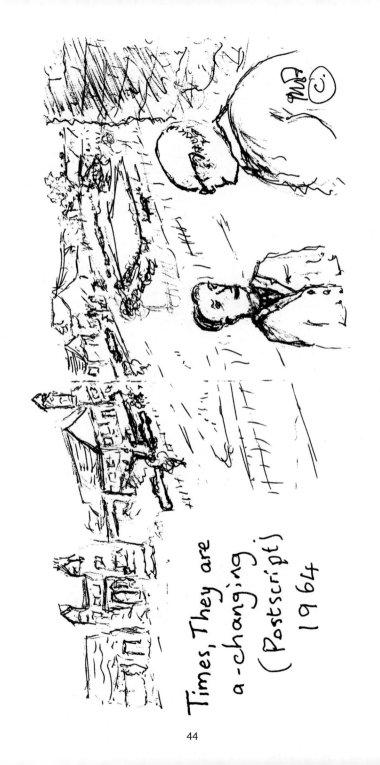

Times, They are
a-changing
(Postscript)
1964

THE TIMES, THEY ARE A'CHANGING
POSTSCRIPT

It is 1964. I am thirty and I have now been teaching at my old school: now "Albert Road Junior School", for about three years. The old school has changed and so has Education in the town. A brand new Secondary Modern School, "St Cyres", has been established and is building a good reputation for itself,

So no more ignominious Forms One and Two, crowded into the top hall of the old Elementary School.

Co-education, boys and girls together, has replaced the old segregation in all but the Grammar School.

Albert Road Junior School is "streamed" into levels of ability, A,B and C Classes plus my class "The Remove". It is a big school with 13 classes to cover the four year-groupings from 7 to 11 year olds.

The Town has been "re-zoned" and now our catchment area has extended southwards to include such "posh" areas as Westbourne and Plymouth Roads, where the "crachach" are deemed to reside. Interestingly the "A" stream classes are almost completely filled with girls, with boys outnumbering them in the "B" and "C" streams. Is it just a co-incidence that the brothers of most of the "A" stream girls attend the local private prep school although there exists a similar private school for girls in Penarth?

On one occasion a fairly wealthy and prominent Penarthian visits the Headteacher to plead that his son be moved from the "B" stream into the "A" class, "if only, for the Social Contacts"!

I discover that the Old Headteacher, now long retired, lives just across the way beyond Belle Vue Park and visit him on my way home. On the doorstep, he gazes at the fleet of large cars drawing up outside our old Elementary School, sighs wistfully and wryly comments:

"FORD, IN OUR DAY IT WAS THE BORSTAL OF PENARTH. NOW IT'S THE ETON!"

TEACHING STAFF AT ALBERT JUNIOR SCHOOL
Summer 1964

(Left to Right):
Rear Row: Les Brookes, Miss Ray, Mrs Davies (Temp), Bert Davies,
Front: Bob Lee, Mike Ford, Morgan Davies, Tom Rees (HeadTeacher),
Mrs Yeoman(Deputy HT), Mrs Rona Harlow, Roy Thorne.

Calendar Month ending 30th APRIL, 19

1st Week ending		2nd Week ending 13th April		3rd Week ending 20th April		4th Week ending 27th April		5th Week ending 30th April		Total days Attendance of Children	Brought Forward	Total for Calendar Quarter 58	CLASS No.
M T W T F	TOTAL	M T W T F	TOTAL	M T W T F	TOTAL	M T W T F	TOTAL	M T W T F	TOTAL				

TOTALS

Details for Calendar Month

Attendances

Times Open { M 16 / A 14 } Total 30

Average 39

Mike Ford

The author was born in Penarth and, now aged 73, has spent all his life save for four years resident in the town. Two years were spent as a National Serviceman, mostly based in Chester and two years as a Student Teacher in a London Teacher Training College. His teaching career started in Barry, followed by 15 years in Penarth and the final 13 years as an Advisory Remedial Teacher in Mid Glamorgan.

This collection of anecdotes and sketches was started in February 2007, intended for his seven grandchildren, although the idea of writing such a series had been forming over many years. The present booklet, "Albert Road Boys First" is intended as only the first in a series entitled "PENARTH, Not the Centre of the Universe, BUT....."

This covers the author's own (mis)adventures in and around Albert Road Elementary School for Boys during the years 1938 - 1945. A second book, covering the years 1934 - 1946 and describing life "On the Home Front" has already been completed and is currently being published. These first two books, complementing each other will, it is hoped, convey to younger readers some idea of what it was like to be a child in Wartime Penarth..... at least in the Northern (Docks) end of the town!

"PENARTH......
Not the Centre of the Universe, BUT.............."

Reminiscences of An Old Penarthian.

2.
"On The Home Front!"
(1934 - 1946)

By MIKE FORD

PENARTH......
Not the Centre of the Universe, BUT.............."

Reminiscences of An Old Penarthian.

2.

"On The Home Front!"

(1934 - 1946)

By MIKE FORD
(Copyright Reserved)

This Book is dedicated to

Sue Hopkins

Dear Friend,
Artist,
Music & Poetry Lover,
Sometime Travelling Companion,
Teacher,
Great Conversationalist,
Humorist
and
(above all)
An Inspiration to all who know her.

^^

Many thanks to Sue for reawakening in me a love of poetry, music and particularly in sketching. It has been only by observing her techniques over the past five years, that I have now had the confidence to attempt to illustrate myself this and all other books in the series. Any (or rather all) shortcomings in this area are solely down to an as yet to be perfected skill. But Sue has shown the way and I add my gratitude to that from all others who have been privileged to have received her tutoring and encouragement,.
Many, Many thanks

"Mam" or "Mum"?

The question of which form of address or referral I was in the habit of using to my own mother was raised by a long standing friend who knew of my family from quite early days. Should I have used the more usual (for Penarth of the times) expression "Mum" in my anecdotes? Or why had I changed this to "Mam", which seemed to her and probably to all others who "knew" the family from my early years, quite out of character. I must admit, had to admit, that at the time I more regularly used "Mum".

BUT, I have given this much thought and make no apologies for sticking to "Mam" (usually although not consistently so). In this collection of family histories and their home settings, I believe that the term "Mam" more accurately reflects the Welsh influence of MAM by the fireside, in her daily toil and her typically "Mam-ish" devotion to her children, particularly the sons (almost akin to that of the Jewish Momma or the Mam as portrayed by Ryan Davies in the TV series "Ryan and Ronnie").

"Know thyself!" is a tall order and probably one best left to old age, when all the influences of one's childhood nurturing can be assessed and incorporated into ones own self image, which anyone else outside immediate family may believe they know accurately, but never really do.

"Anglo-Welsh" may be a better description of many a character in South East Wales. Indeed, how gifted and universally recognised would the achievements of many have been without the contribution of that peculiarly idiosyncratic Welsh cultural background (you know the ones I mean: writers, poets, actors)?

It is more often the posturing of some of our "pillars of the community" who draw down the more striking and justified ridicule by their "non partisan" but noticeable disdain of all things "too Welsh!" The following apocryphal description of one of Penarth's cultural events of the not too distant past may illustrate this perfectly:

Occasion: First Official Public Reception of the first ever official visit by Civic Leaders of St. Pol de Leon, Penarth's twin town in Brittany.
Setting: Front Lawn of West House (Penarth's Town Hall)

The Breton visitors have finished a rendition of a Breton Folk song – in their own language and now invite Penarth's Town Councillors:
"Please could YOU now sing us something typically Welsh?"
Penarth Town Councillors looking worried but eventually step forward confidently and burst into a hearty rendering of:

> "Oh, We do like to be beside the sea-side,
> We do like to be beside the sea!"

As Dylan had one of his characters, the Rev Eli Jenkins, say with true Welsh Hwyl:

"Thank God, we are a musical nation!"

FOREWORD
"I Remember, I Remember, the house where I was born"

This, the second book in the Series "Penarth....not The Centre of the Universe, BUT.............", covers much the same period as the first: "Albert Road Boys First", but against that book's treatment of (L.M.F.) Little Mickey Ford's Elementary School days (Primary School, nowadays), .I now deal with "On the Home Front"....the not (just) yet ended saga of the life and times of L.M.F. from cradle to........... well, not quite that far, YET. .....So. L.M.F.... the early years at home and at play, it is then. (Don't yawn, Rhys... it's not all boring, b-o-r-i-n-g !)

The modern generation of kids (Tut, Tut..."children", Mr. Ford, **Children**"), are much the same as we were, though a young Mum recently smiled sweetly at me and knowingly said: "Ah, but you don't understand modern children, Mike. They are so much more mature."

Read on and see if you agree !

I must admit I had the great advantage of being born into a home, which despite its comparative material poverty was rich in every other way: in love, self-sacrifice and most relevant, I believe in this modern age...a world where many adults, particularly parents, had time for children....treated them with respect and gave of themselves, the greatest gift of all, their time and their undivided attention!

So, as Mrs Helen Chick added laughingly to my observation: "Modern Youth think they invented the wheel. They didn't! WE did!"..."Yes, Mike, and now they're riding on it!" We both laughed.
Well, that's about enough for a Foreword, folks.
Read! Enjoy (I hope)! and look out for the next book(s) I hope to write and illustrate before that old man with the big scythe comes along!

Ciao! (See, I'm still "with it" if only just)
Mike ......my "grown up monica" but still, at heart,: L.M.F.!

AKNOWLEDGEMENTS

Thanks to:
Wally Davies of Sully: For kind permission to use, for the cover, his photo of my
father, Pop, leading "Prince" out from the stables at "Seaview", Penarth (40s/50s ?).
Clive Francis: For kind permission to use, for inclusion in "Special Treats for Wartime
Kids", the group photo of children at the Firemen's Childrens' Xmas Party in 1944 (?)
My Sister Bea: For painstakingly proof reading the original manuscripts.
My Brother Jack: For correcting factual errors and contributing, as did Bea, additional family information and supplementary material.
Emma of 'Hi-Plan' Office Services: For patient advice and technical help.
Thanks also to all those Penarthians, too numerous to list: Who have offered advice and encouragement and particularly to those whose practical help and use of contacts may lead to these memoirs getting published.
Diolch yn fawr iawn!

CONTENTS

This book covers the period 1934 to 1946.
It's hoped to continue this series with further Memoirs.

"The Scene" is Set
(Imminent Arrival)
January 1934.

WFC
2007

62.1

8

THE SCENE IS SET

It is January 1934. My arrival is imminent and my father, two brothers and three sisters wait anxiously by Mam's bedside. If all goes well, I will be the eighth child to be born at home, No 26 Pembroke Terrace, Penarth. Two infant siblings have died before me, leaving a gap of almost ten years between me and nine year old, Bea; twelve between me and George; fourteen between myself and Enid; sixteen years separate me from Jack, my eldest brother and eighteen from Violet: the eldest of all.

Dad was born in Penarth and has two sisters also living above a corner grocery shop just a few streets away. Granddad, who hailed from the Somerset village of Cokesly between Bath and Glastonbury also lives not far away. Granddad came to South Wales as part of that great migration from the West Country to South Wales and had been a stone mason, helping build the big houses of the wealthy in Penarth: shipowners and others who had richly benefited from the importance of "King Coal"...black diamonds to some.

Mam had been part of a mining family in Llanhilleth, near Abertillery in the valleys of Monmouthshire. At thirteen years of age she had started work "in service" as a lowly housemaid to one of these wealthy households.

Family history has it that she met Dad on the Esplanade during one of her half-days "off". There had been some commotion as a poor wretch had committed suicide by jumping from Penarth Pier and somehow they met up.
They were a devoted couple but ensnared by near poverty and a commitment to their children and to the small greengrocery business and market garden which helped support them, they would be unable to take a holiday together until they were in their eighties.
But the morrow, 25th, would bring one more mouth to feed.

"Mother's Milk"

January 1934

6.3.07

ENTER LITTLE MICKEY FORD

The story (for him) begins.........

How far back can you remember ?

In no way comparing myself (a mere scribbler) with the great Sir John Betjeman,
I do nevertheless claim to have, like him, a very early memory – recollection of infancy.

But I do claim to go one better than the venerable Sir John He claimed that he could remember
quite clearly having been bounced very heavily in his pram over a pavement curbstone by his
careless Nanny.

I can remember, albeit fuzzily (and in sound only) the gentle and pacifying words being most
lovingly whispered into my tender ear: " Do you want some more ? ".
Of course there is an unmistakable context to these words and they, for me, represent the loving
caring home and the solicitous protection of two of the most wonderful parents a child could ever
wish for.

The family circumstances were fairly impoverished....almost living from hand to mouth. The Great
Depression had scarcely ceased to hold its grip – particularly on most of the inhabitants of the
North (Docks) end of Penarth.

Moreover, family tragedy had struck...not just once but twice....prior to my birth.
I was to be the eighth (and last child) of Mary Rebecca Ford. But little Ritchie and little Jean, Nos Six
and Seven had died in Infancy....one from Diptheria, the other from scalds, sustained from an upset
cauldron of boiling water. Although large families and Infant Mortality were not uncommon in
those days, every such family tragedy was still and felt keenly as an enormous loss.

Hence, I believe, from the very beginning I was very much overprotected (as my later stories will
further show). I have the suspicion that I may not have been fully weaned until the age of fifteen or
sixteen !!!

"Do you want some more ?" False memory syndrome ? Maybe.
But even if, unlike Sir John's more reliable recollection of being savagely buffeted by a careless
Nanny, my recollection is deemed suspect by you, Dear Reader, those impressions were just a
portent of things to come and of the simple loving character of my Dear Mother and, later, of my
Dear Father which I hope to illustrate in the stories yet to be written.

Would that all modern children received the unstinting attention, the devotion and noble example
of those simple, near poverty-stricken but stoic and uncomplaining
Parents I had the great privilege of having been welcomed into the world by!

"Welcome Home!"

"WELCOME HOME"

The basement front room was the warmest and homeliest room in the house. For most of the year a big fire burnt in the old Welsh Fire Range and it was in this room that most of the home scenes of childhood were played out, the warmth of Mam's care felt and that of all the many welcome visitors too. But most welcome always, which as a toddler I remember, were Pop's homecomings, particularly when he carried in to my great glee that big old potato sack on his back, with its lumpy protuberances proclaiming the presence of varied shaped wooden offcuts amongst all the wood shavings, intended for our horse's stable bedding. Then, Pop had obviously hurried home from Price the Joiner's works in Station Road and he had me in mind when he buried these strangely shaped wooden blocks in amongst the wood shavings.

Mam would often play with me and my makeshift blocks on the carpet before the fire and the imaginative games we played and the foreign lands we visited in our fantasies linger in the memory even now. Pop's large oilskin raincoat made a wonderful ship to be sailed across dividing seas and even some of the adult visitors would join in the fun.

Brother George, next youngest in the family to me, would often play too either indoors or out in our tiny back garden, but my ears would be alert for the sound of Pop's returning voice.

"Salad Days" and The Young Ones 1938/39

© USR.

SALAD DAYS AND "THE YOUNG ONES"

In those pre-war years, I always seemed to be surrounded by busy, happy people. Home seemed to buzz with chatter, laughter, noise. If not Mam and the delicious aromas of cooking accompanied by the sound of the knife on the chopping board, heralding mint sauce and lamb for Sunday dinner, then the clink of teacups as customers or lorry drivers also partook of whatever was on offer. I was never, ever lonely.

Sunday mornings, unless I was off with Pop somewhere or other, often meant The Young Ones tumbling uproariously down the outside stone steps into our basement living room to play an equally uproarious board game which I didn't understand at all but seemed to involve moving silver tokens around the outside of the board, thrusting wads of pretend money at each other and carefully placing tiny green or larger red house shaped pieces of painted wood on the inside edges of the coloured squares around the border of the board. There would be groans, yells of triumph and much horseplay and I too from my elevated position on the fireside armchair would grin and chuckle even though I could never fully understand what all the fuss was about. The clowning and antics of my brothers Jack and George and their two friends, Sid Draper and David Coppock drew me into their world of fun, youth and laughter.

From time to time, Mam would appear with cups of tea and maybe some cake ....even sandwiches if the game went on for hours ....which it usually did.

In my mind's eye, I can still see that scene of hilarity with the sun streaming down through our large basement sash windows and four fit and lively young ones sprawled out on the carpet before me like some Rabelaisian tale illustrated by whatsisname (you know, that chap who painted glorious mediaeval panoramic scenes of hunters returning to their village in winter) or maybe by Renoir with those artists' River Café parties. Take your pick.

Later on but Sundays still, the Young Ones would no doubt stroll along Penarth's Monkey Run, The Esplanade, where generations of teenagers would stroll up and down, up and down, to eye the girls and vice versa, as I would do much later. Then, probably with the traditional, come-hitherish ploy of the poseur, Penguin book on display in outside pocket, poetic and mysterious, the lads might stroll up the far hill and along the cliff walk.

Little did we suspect that two of those happily frolicking Young Ones would have their lives prematurely wrenched from them in the coming war.

Playmates
and
Street Games

PLAYMATES AND STREET GAMES

For some years, I was the only boy living in our street. Girls, girls, girls! Maybe I would have welcomed this if I had been a teenager, but as a six, seven or even ten year old it meant that, unless I went looking for other lads in The Triangle or further afield, it was girls I always seemed to be playing with. There were even two of them lodging in our house with their parents, Mr and Mrs Caine from London. Mr Caine was a soldier at the same Ack-Ack Battery as my sister, Enid. Eileen, at about 7 and the elder, was very pretty but Ann, being only about 5, not noticeable.

Both, however, looked to me as a handy playmate. As did Pauline next door and the other girls in the street. And so I quickly learned all the girls' games of hopscotch, "Jack across the Water" "Who's got the ball-ee-O" and all the other "cissy"games, as my mates would call them. And so it didn't do my "street cred" much good either.

This, coupled with the fact that Pop was usually out "on the land" all day so my only companions at home were Mam and my two surviving sisters meant that my self-image was always rather more feminine than male-macho. To make matters worse, my sisters had discovered my uses in helping get them ready for dances, etc. I became a "dab-hand" at applying mud face-masks, bathing feet and attending to toe-nails! This again contrasted with the hurly burly of our rough and ready Albert Road Elementary School where preparation in trench-warfare or unarmed combat would have been more appropriate.

But just occasionally some other lads would wander into this realm of fair maidens. Usually quite accidentally, chasing a run-away hoop or, totally absorbed in their game of marbles, rounding the corner from Albert Road, seemed not to notice me or assumed me to be just another "girlie" and beneath their contemptuous regard.

Just sometimes, a lad came along from The Triangle with a length of rope, clambered the gas street lamp-post and I could join him in swinging round and round, clonking shins and elbows against the metal but feeling quite manly under the girls' admiring gazes.

A couple of other pastimes should be mentioned which reflect the wartime background of the time. To make model 'planes, we would melt down in an old tin can, odd scraps of lead pipe and in clay moulds made from the greyish brown clay dug out of the bank where the sea cadet hut was or had just started to be built and scraping out the rough shape of a spitfire, cast the hot fluid lead into this, leaving it to cool and set. As we became more skilled we would even try to make toy soldiers, ships and other objects of warfare, to play with indoors on wet days.

The other popular item was a model tank made from an old wooden cotton reel, piece of candle, elastic band and short stick. With the reel's edges cut into serrated teeth and the elastic band unwinding and turning the stick, lubricated against the cotton reel by the short piece of candle, it could slowly climb over all sorts of obstacles and we played at tank battles and races..

Just occasionally the stern disapproving old man living opposite would be enthused enough to join us and show us a street game from a former era, "bat and rat"(?), with a short carefully shaped piece of wood, pointed at both ends which he demonstrated by sharply hitting one end and as it flew upwards, batting it in mid-air to see how far he could get it.

"IT WAS LIFE, JIM, BUT NOT AS WE (NOW) KNOW IT!"

"BULLET" ("BULLA"), AND "AN ACT OF TREASON"

It was soon to be my birthday and I had been given some money. I had five shillings to spare (now about 25 new pence, but in those days quite a considerable sum for a child and even for an adult probably about one quarter of a day's pay).

Decisions, decisions! What to buy? Someone living not far away had had a new litter of puppies born to their bitch. Mongrels, of course, but each going for just five shillings. No contest! I would buy a puppy, went to choose and chose the liveliest of the bunch. Though a bit strange in its appearance, a rough haired terrier/dachshund cross, it was very appealing. And so I now had a dog.

Next question: what should I call it ?

Seeing it streak off after a cat, no problem ! It was wartime and it seemed to run as fast as a bullet, so it should be called just that: "Bullet".

The trouble was that when you tried to call it repeatedly back from a fight or a cat chase, it was hard to call out fast enough and in full the word, "Bullet ! Bullet! Bullet !" You try it ! See what I mean ?

And so his name had to change, be made shorter and so it became, "Bulla ! Bulla ! Bulla!"

And THEN a friend (?) pointed out that a "dachshund" was a German dog and that as there was a war on and as my two brothers were in the RAF helping fight against the Germans it was not very nice, to say the least, to have bought an "enemy dog"!

I worried a lot about this and wrote a letter to my brother Jack, who was out in the Middle East to apologize for this terrible act of treason, But after a while and since the soldiers, sailors 'an airmen in the NAAFI in the basement of Albert Road Methodist Church invited me in with Bulla, and they seemed to like him, anyway, I forgot about it until years later I found that letter of apology to brother Jack.

At the
Allotment:
Bunching Radishes
1944 — 45? 50?

BUNCHING RADISHES

Pop, besides being a greengrocer and a carter, also had an allotment.

We preferred to call it "a smallholding", and even on my birth-certificate "father's occupation" is given as "market gardener".

The "small holding", just a few acres or so, was rented from the Marquis of Bute Estates and had for decades previously been part of Cardiff City's extensive tipping area for the city's household refuse, which by now had rotted down and created a quite fertile if very soft growing area. It lay in a bend of the River Ely, overlooked by Leckwith Woods and not far from the pumping station and The Toll Gate, also owned by the Marquis of Bute, which levied tolls on all users of Penarth Road and was not closed until the mid '50s.

Bounded by the River Ely and alongside by dilapidated home-made buildings of piggeries, there was also a plentiful ready supply of manure to be dug in with the aid of the rusting old plough which lay about for most of the year awaiting the autumn visit of Pop's carthorse.

In summer, the plagues of horseflies tormented us and the fetid aroma of pig-dung clung to us and to our clothes until we got home, worn out and stinking, with the setting sun.

Amongst the many fairly popular and productive crops were radishes and so Pop would buy his seed from the merchant, Noah, Rees and Griffin in Grangetown at the corner of Penarth Road and Blaen-Clydach Street, not of course in small packets but loose, by the quarter and half pound.

From Spring until Summer, on many evenings I would be called on to travel by bus to The Toll Gate and spend several hours pulling and then bunching radishes, chosen from the long low rows and then washed in the barrel of rainwater by the tumbledown corrugated iron shed, tied with raffia and stacked neatly into the old Wm. Bradnum box or laid out into neat rows in shallow wooden tomato trays.

If it were a Friday evening the filled boxes were left behind the shed, ready for the Saturday early morn's collection by us with the horse and cart en route for Cardiff Market and Custom-House Street.

On other days, I would carry maybe just one tray home by bus.

While other boys were perhaps kicking a tin can or old scruffy tennis ball around streets or patches of waste ground back in Penarth and learning the basics of football or cricket, here I was – on my own, out "in the wilderness" (from a "townie" child's point of view) but now, in retrospect, just part of the rich total experience of being "Pop's" youngest son.

On the Home Front
The joys of cleaning a split-level, terraced, house!

"Sitting Out"
(cleaning windows)
and
"Swilling" the Scullery Floor

26 Pembroke Terrace
:- every weekend 19?? -1970

© MJ7. 10·3·07

"HOME, SWEET HOME"

For all of us, Number 26, Pembroke Terrace, was just this, "Home, Sweet Home", and here the family or at least Mam and Pop stayed for over sixty years, but it was really Mam , like Mams everywhere, who really created this warm atmosphere of home.

But it has to be admitted that, in those days, it was one hell of a house to maintain and keep clean. Of course, in those days not many labour saving devices existed and with the additional burden for Mam of the dirt and grime from a greengrocery business being run from home with six surviving children to care for, it was her uncomplaining efforts and unfailing spirit that kept us all afloat.

The split-level terraced house, one of a block of four built on the hillside overlooking Cardiff Bay, had steps everywhere: two stone steps from the short front pathway from the street to enter the house, by way of the front door and even then, after a short length of corridor passing front and "middle" rooms, three steps down into the (later) bathroom and kitchen.

Back at the front of the house, immediately inside the gate one went down a flight of stone steps to reach the basement courtyard and, passing the large bayed window of the front basement living room, one passed under the archway of the path above, past the coal-house on one's left to enter the house by the basement front door, along the corridor past the high wooden screed and curtained doorway of the living room, through a glass panelled door into the gloom of a further stretch of corridor, passing the dark stairway to upstairs on left and rear kitchen on right and arriving at three steps down to a flag-stoned scullery, where the fruit and veg were kept. Steps did not end there!

Going through the external door on the right, one went down three stone steps to the small rear courtyard, at the end of which between the towering walls of our and the neighbour's homes to reach three more steps down into the small patch of garden and, at the end of the garden path, one met another three steps down to the garden doorway opening onto the rear lane.

I will not describe the upper floors where the bedrooms were and the stairways to reach them. My sketch, I think, will give you an idea of the awkwardness of this house for any housewife, let alone any woman with the additional trials for our Mam, already mentioned.

Mam "sat out" to clean the outside of the sash windows, lowering the upper window onto her lap while perching herself on the windowsills with the topmost windows meaning she "sat out" above a potential drop of about forty feet ! This she did regularly until well into old age. I tried it once myself but never again. It was terrifying.

My only regular job in the house was, from age about twelve until nineteen when I left home, to "swill down" ,with buckets of cold water from the only tap above the bosh, the flag-stoned scullery floor at the end of Saturday's "Round" after I had sorted out and stacked the fruit and veg.

It was a terrible house for Mam to work, but nevertheless she made it "Home, Sweet Home".

Pop: cleaning fish at "the bosh"
in the scullery. (Sometime 1944–46) B2.

©MJT
10.3.02

"THE SCULLERY"

Looking back now, with hindsight, the living and working conditions and facilities around the house were almost Dickensian. But this was a different era, which perhaps for some lasted much longer into modern times. Indeed when my brother Jack had returned after the war, he began energetically trying to improve the house for Mam. It took some years to do this and The Scullery, the most primitive room, was high on the list but not until the mid fifties did its turn come and, a planning application to convert part of the basement into an additional bathroom having been made, the Town's Surveyor visited to view. I well remember the look of amazement on his face at the sight of all the fruit, veg and other assorted objects, albeit stacked neatly, and with a scrubbed but broken flagstone floor. Poor fellow must have had almost a heart attack but no doubt felt out of his element, probably more used to enjoying all the advantages of a then modern home.

Pop spent a good deal of time here when not on his allotment or tending his horse. Here he weighed out the fruit and vegetable needs of various housewives and landladies of small B & Bs then carried them to their doors on weekdays. He also sold rabbits, sometimes poultry and regularly: fish.

He would skin, gut and clean the rabbits, cut and fillet the fish over the bosh, using its solitary cold tap to cleanse everything.

Mam also did her clothes washing here, using an old gas water boiler to heat water for the washing and a large tin bath outside in the rear courtyard to scrub the clothes on a wash board, before finally rinsing them under the cold tap, wringing out by hand the excess water and then hanging them out to dry on the line high above the tiny garden.

The scullery was in effect the workshop of our small business, "Open All Hours", and the scene of much activity, both domestic and commercial. The Surveyor may have returned home with scandalised tales for his family and friends, but for many people in the North of Penarth this was our very life and the only way to survive. And The Scullery was the engine room for us to do so.

"MARY! "POP" Where's the Diamond

© MDL March 2007

"MARY, WHERE'S THE DIAMOND?"

Pop was always a great one for his tea. He would drink three or four big "breakfast cups" of it at a sitting and I lost count of the number of times a day he would stop for tea, (Mind you he wouldn't take long about it, and he was hard at work from dawn until dusk putting our meals on the table, so no one could begrudge him that.)

But he loved it very sweet too. If sugar was about (usually on rations) he'd take three or four spoonfuls in each cup.

The trouble was that there was only one teaspoon in the whole house, or so he claimed.

So, when frustrated in his search for the one and only teaspoon, this was what he would usually shout to Mam, who was somewhere busily working in one of the rooms of our huge and awkward house with its many split levels.

His shout of **"MARY, WHERE'S THE DIAMOND?"** would re-echo, seemingly for minutes around the house, and years later – after seeing some of Stanley Spencer's paintings of very realistic resurrection scenes and pondering on them, I became sure that Dear old Pop may still be shouting it in the family grave in nearby St Augustine's churchyard.

Pop's
Bedtime
"at the
Terrace"

The Echo

POP'S BEDTIME AT THE TERRACE

Pop, "son of the soil" as he was and working from before dawn to dusk on the allotment, caring for his horse in the ramshackle stable in Windsor Terrace Lane, carrying orders on foot from our basement greengrocer's shop and on and on and on - he finally went to bed, according to the season, sometimes quite early, but always exhausted. Anyway, Pop never wore a watch but nevertheless he was a good judge of what the time was.

But downstairs in the basement sitting room, however tired he was at the end of the day, he had time for little Mickey, his eighth and last child. Sitting by the old fire range with its brightly burning fire, he would take off his tie and collar, his old worn but cleaned-every-day leggings and boots, pick up the Echo and settle into the sagging armchair, welcoming with outstretched arms and a broad grin little Mickey, who then clambered up onto Pop's lap to snuggle down and gently fall asleep there. Pop would give a contented sigh while struggling to read his paper around the child's small drooping head. .

At last, Pop was ready for bed. Softly calling Mam's attention and waiting while she lifted away the now sleeping Mickey, he only then got his candle* and his unfinished Echo, his smeared, one armed old spectacles and started the long climb up three flights of stairs to bed. Once in bed, he lay on his side with the Echo held precariously near the candle. Sometimes, downstairs we would hear from on high a loud yell and a frantic clapping of hands. Mam would smile and knowingly comment, "He's done it again ! ... fallen asleep and let the Echo drop on the candle" Mickey joined in her chuckle.

Sometimes at night, Mam would hear him mumbling in his sleep about where he might get horseradish growing wild up in Leckwith Woods and get as much as a shilling a stick for them, particularly at Passover, in Cardiff Market. Times were hard and Pop, though poor was proud and always concerned with looking after his family's needs. He had once gone to the Parish Relief Board, but felt so humiliated that he had sworn that he would never go there again. Times were hard, but his family were never failed by him.

---

*The Candle. Even after electricity was installed, Pop continued to use a candle. Downstairs in the sitting room, as night fell, Pop would sit in the gloaming until someone entered and only then would he ask timoursly, in a West Country brogue (though born locally in Salop Place)

"Will you ON the light for me?"
I think this apprehension and fear of modern gadgetry affected me too and still does.....the technophobe that I continue to bee. (blast this stupid 'pooter thing!)

MUM 1932.....1970
and the Sunday Night Customers

The World

March 2007

30

MAM AND THE SUNDAY NIGHT CUSTOMERS

Running a small family "business" from home meant "Open All Hours".

And if Pop was off working on the allotment (smallholding of about an acre, rented from the Marquis of Bute Estates), Dear Mam, besides cleaning an awkward split level three storey house, caring for growing and adolescent children, served customers with fruit and vegetables from the three-steps' down, flag-stoned scullery at the end of the corridor.

Often it happened on a Sunday late evening, maybe Pop having gone. exhausted to bed, that a few more women friends would call for a few things from the scullery. Mam would offer them tea and cake and leave them for a while to chat or play with sleepy young me until I too would doze off in the battered old armchair.

I would be vaguely aware of the continuing chatter, the clinking of teacups as more tea and more cake were dispensed. Then, probably after I had been safely tucked up in bed, Mam would accompany home those ladies who were afraid of going home alone in the dark.

The Ford family "business' never really flourished or ever became the basis of a commercial empire but it was certainly popular in our part of Penarth and the house seemed to be always full of friendly people, warmth and the buzz of conversation, laughter and care.

It was and still is, if only in memory now, a land of warm dreams, hope and promise.

Homeward Bound
with soft fruit
Summer 1944ish

© MyD

"HOMEWARD-BOUND WITH SOFT FRUIT"

On his allotment, Pop had many, many soft-fruit bushes: blackcurrants, redcurrants and gooseberries. I never counted them, but always thought that there were a hundred or more. And of course, in season, there was much work to be done, picking.

I spent many summer evenings and school holidays doing this, travelling to the Toll Gate by bus with an empty basket or two and settling down on an upturned box and moving from bush to bush until the baskets were full.

Then, grimy, sweating and probably stinking from the cloying aromas of the surrounding piggeries and rotting detritus of suburban Cardiff's ash-bins , which had formed these allotments for decades before, I would start home-ward with the filled baskets.

Next to the Toll-Gate's window-fronted gate-keeper's booth stood large advertising hoardings, in the middle of which was an alcove where a cold water tap was placed for travellers to refresh themselves. Here I would slake my thirst before crossing the road to wait by the furthermost huge white painted toll-gate.

And wait...and wait.....and wait. If lucky, I might be able to get on the first bus to come along from Cardiff, en route for Penarth.

But sometimes, depending on the hour, a number of buses crowded with home going office-workers would pass me by.

Their faces pressed against the windows, they would gaze at me with curiosity.
And even when I managed to get on, they would stare. Sometimes, I might even hear an admiring comment about the fruit I was carrying. But always, as my not-too-fragrant scent pervaded the air, I would become self-consciously aware of my erstwhile friendly companions shrinking away from me and becoming unnaturally voluble in their own conversations or finding fascinating objects to stare at outside the bus as it rumbled Penarth-wards.

I never really overcame this feeling of being some sort of social pariah and almost felt as if I should carry a bell with me and, entering the bus, shout "Unclean ! Unclean !"

But the succulent fruit pies and jams that Mam made soon had me forget my embarrassment very quickly!

P.Y.O (Pick your Own)
Neighbours Co-op. 1940-50

"P.Y.O. NEIGHBOURS' CO-OP"

Many people nowadays think that "P.Y.O" ("Pick Your Own"- fruit, vegetables, etc) is a fairly modern idea. "The Guardian" newspaper only recently produced a supplement on the subject with its lead-writer reminiscing about his childhood in the sixties, the delights of "P.Y.O." and wanting to introduce his own children to this entertaining and healthy occupation. I beg to differ. That is, in that it is a relatively modern concept.

This practice must have happened over decades before the sixties, if not centuries. Amongst small-holders and poorer market gardeners at least it had long been the practice to invite neighbours to help pick their crops of soft fruit and, in lieu of payment, to take a share of what they had picked. Unable to afford to hire pickers, there was no other way for such growers to harvest their fruit.

On our allotment, or smallholding, half-way between Penarth and Cardiff next to the River Ely and rented from the Marquis of Bute Estates, it was always the practice to carry on our harvesting in this way. The women neighbours would catch a bus to The Toll Gate (also owned by the Marquis) and armed with baskets, bottles of cold tea, bread and cheese, they would perch themselves for hours on end on old upturned wooden boxes beside the bushes of gooseberries, black- and red-currants, perspiring with bowed backs aching and warding off the plagues of horseflies from the ramshackle adjacent piggeries. Mam seemed particularly attractive to them and many were the ballooning leg bites she suffered.

At day's end, all retreated homeward and after the weighing of their respective baskets, and receiving their allotted share of the crop, all seemed content although exhausted and usually ready to repeat the experience if more of the crop remained on the bushes.

Yes, THIS was P.Y.O., if not as we (now) know it!

"WHOSE PARTY IS IT, ANYWAY?"

Sister Enid and I were not always the best of friends.

Admittedly, she had arrived or rather returned from "away" after several years and at my tender age in a largish family with all the hustle and bustle of our "open all hours" family business, it took me a long time to work out exactly who she was!

I was to learn later that, in hard times and much to the annoyance of the then Headmistress of Penarth County Grammar School for Girls, she left school before taking her School Certificate to look for work. She was directed to secretarial training and work in Sparkbrooke, Birmingham. Hence, I believe we started off badly, mutually suspicious and many were the confrontations then. In later years, I came to know and love my sister and appreciate all her qualities of generosity, concern and fortitude. But then, was then.

On the outbreak of war, Enid had joined the women's army, the A.T.S. and had a "home posting", living at home, but cycling daily to Lower Penarth, sometimes followed by Bulla, our dog, down to the camp on the hill with its view of the Channel, towards which the anti-aircraft guns were pointed for practice. One of her comrades brought his family down from London to live with us.

From time to time, there were jollifications. Other friends of Enid's were invited for a meal.

However, I clearly remember the day when seeing Enid making most elaborate preparations, carefully spreading out a large white tablecloth, getting plates-full of scrumptious cakes ready and loads of other mysterious foodstuffs that I became convinced that this was going to be some party, but what was the special occasion and as many parents, even now, will recognize, kids only slowly become sure of the sequences of seasons, months and dates – even of their own birthdays.

And so I was convinced too and so convincing must I have been of this as a FACT, that I convinced my Infant School Teacher and a group of friends that indeed it WAS my birthday! And so about half-a dozen of us were let out of school early. My pals dashed home, to scrub up and get their Mams to rummage through cupboards and find something appropriate as a "prezzie".

Congregating noisily and with great anticipation around the top of the steps, we gazed down hungrily at the visible feast which Enid was just putting the last touches to. "Cor, crisps 'an cakes ' an.... funny sort of lemonade in them bottles, innit? Still, s'pose iss some'ink speshull, eh, Mickey ?"

But Sister Enid, catching sight of us and guessing at my mistake, yelled out fiercely, "GO HOME! IT'S NOT HIS BIRTHDAY!"

Reluctantly they turned to me asking belligerently "Whose birthday is it, anyway?"

Even more reluctantly I returned into their outstretched hands the "prezzies", which included a much treasured hoarded pound bar of chocolate. And Arthur, Billy'Edge, Graham Hudd and the others ran off to the Triangle – probably to eat that chocolate.

Meanwhile, still red in the face and unbelieving, I crept down to the backroom kitchen to have another look at that wall calendar and check if it wasn't Enid who had made the mistake.

PENARTH DOCTORS.

"THE PANEL" and arrival of N.H.S.

1948

1942

"LOCAL DOCTORS"

Before the arrival of the National Health Service, it was of course possible to get medical help either by paying privately or by joining a local "Panel" by which scheme one paid a small weekly amount as a form of health insurance. There were naturally wide differences in the kind and quality of service a sick person received, even further exacerbated by the choice of doctor one was attended by.

My Aunts, owners of a corner shop, were able to pay. Hence the rotund rather florid medic who would arrive in his luxurious limousine and would unctuously flutter and flatter his way, waddling in through the side door in King Street to attend either of my aunts who needed his attention and, most importantly, could pay "cash on the nail".

By contrast, my sister Violet who needed his help had to visit his surgery, usually accompanied by my sister Enid. Violet, who was a hairdresser on the large staff of "Poirettes", whose premises were in Stanwell Road, opposite West House (and still used by a hairdressing business) had been unwell for almost a year and worryingly becoming even worse with extremely distressing symptoms. Despite Enid's pleas for an X-Ray to be arranged this had been continually postponed until, almost a year later, she again visited the good doctor and managed to persuade him to do so. A short while later Enid was contacted urgently to make an appointment for Violet and herself to visit the surgery.

There, after she had again been examined, Violet was asked to wait outside while the good doctor spoke gravely to Enid. He regretted to have to tell her that Violet, aged about 24, had only a few weeks to live! Violet died of TB in 1942.

I well remember the foggy evening when I went with Enid in search of The Bed Rest which was available around the town to ease the last sufferings of any dying patient.

By contrast, by the time of arrival of the N.H.S, we had transferred to be patients of Dr Lindsay whose surgery and home were in "Westcross", No 10, Stanwell Road. He was a most caring and concerned doctor with whom all the family stayed for the whole of his working life and from whom many generations of Penarthians received.most attentive and professional help. He was also a famous "character" in Penarth, with a remarkable background. He had been awarded the Military Cross during World War 1, but now drove around town attending patients wearing his carpet slippers and was well known and loved for his great sense of humour as well as his dedication.

I well remember calling on my way to Grammar School and leaving the crowded waiting room to enter his surgery, to be greeted with the cheery words in his soft Irish accent:
"Ahhr , Moikul m'boy. Come on in an' tell me how yo'rr gettin' on with the rugby!"

To my nervous protests that there were a lot of patients waiting, he replied:
"Ahhr, Don't botherr about thaat. Anyway the next is only some old biddy wanting her monkey-gland injection. She wants to stay young frever! Sit down! Sit down! Sure, The Rugby's far more imporrtant!"

The (Saturday) Daytime Air-raid

© 2007 大丈

THE SATURDAY DAYTIME AIR-RAID

It was Saturday again and the important "Round" of Penarth about to begin. The horse was waiting impatiently, pawing the tarmac of Pembroke Terrace and striking sparks off the road with its metal - shod hooves. Suddenly the banshee wailing of the town's air-raid warning siren broke the peaceful chatter of some waiting customers clustered around the laden cart.

Pausing only to put a feed-bag over the horse's head and secure the brake and chocks under the wheels, Pop pushed me towards the outside stone steps leading down to our basement before following Mrs H. one of the customers also. The others had run off to their nearby homes.

Mam and sister Bea, pale and fearful, hurried me and Mrs H. along the corridor to take shelter in the big cupboard below the stairs. Bulla, our mongrel dog, eagerly followed Mrs H., while Mam , Bea and I went into a protective huddle.

I had always been intrigued by the odd way Bulla behaved whenever he caught sight or sound of Mrs H. He seemed to go wild even before he saw her whenever the sound of Mrs H's high-pitched voice was to be heard. She was a small, slight lady and quite excitable herself but even she would become embarrassed as did my sisters whenever Bulla leapt at her, squealing with delight as he wrapped his legs around hers and moved in an odd sort of fashion. I didn't understand my sisters' explanation that Bulla "had a pash" for Mrs H.. Or even why they would explain no more than that, going red as they refused.

Still, more things to worry about now as the low throb of the overhead planes' engines became audible, coming closer and closer most threateningly. And what about the poor horse up there still in the street?

Pop must have been worrying about him too as he edged towards the door to peep upwards from time to time.

But at last, the sound of the planes quietened away and the welcome "All Clear" of the siren brought our thoughts back to the day to come and "The Round". We rushed up the stone stairway to find the horse safe and sound, still munching away at his chaff. Almost ready to go.

At that moment, I heard my sister's yell: "Bulla! Let go of Mrs H.!"

XMAS CONCERT 1942

ACK-ACK CO.

WARTIME SPECIAL TREATS

For all children, it seemed, wartime brought extra treats in that any organisation with which one's adult relatives were involved in made a special effort to include the children in their festivities.

And so, with sister Enid, serving at the Lower Penarth unit of an Anti Aircraft Battery, I was invited to go to a Camp Christmas Concert, part musical, part children's party.

What the musical was, I cannot now remember, except that there were scenes of fishermen and their womenfolk and us being urged to join in the singing of choruses. One song, I do remember, was of "Pedro the Fisherman".

It may not have been on the same occasion, so I may be just indulging my imagination in including several adults standing in the aisle but based on sister Enid's recounting of her experience, having proudly witnessed the adulation of her camp commandant, a major (or perhaps another "Captain Mannering") for brother George, visiting in his bewinged RAF uniform. Comrades in Arms, I suppose.

Another special treat was that provided by the local A.F.S. (Auxiliary Fire Service). And, my Uncle Joe being a part-time fireman, I enjoyed the fringe benefits too.

Another childhood friend, Clive Francis, reminded me of this by showing me a group photo taken of all the children present at another Xmas party, organised by the A.F.S. at the local Church Hall.

Also, by courtesy of the A.F.S. was a summer fete at Barry Island. Here in a field behind the shops opposite the fairground, we were entertained by firemen's competitions and displays, while ice-cream, cakes and pop was given to the kids while thirsty adults congregated in the beer tent.

These events, punctuated by Church Whitsun Treats with their lorry loads of church-pew seated kids transported to places like "The Trolley Lines", gave us a taste of carefree, almost pre-war, merriment, sponsored by our ever-attentive grown-ups.

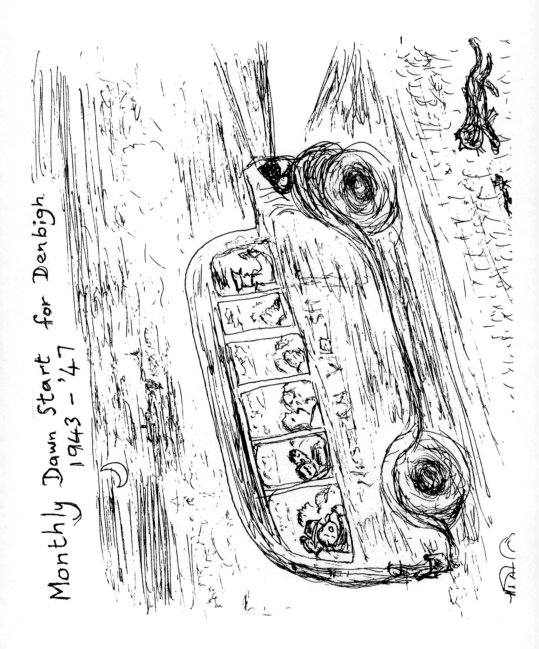

Monthly Dawn Start for Denbigh
1943 – '47

44

DAWN START FOR DENBIGH

A year after sister, Violet, died of TB, sister Enid was also diagnosed as having this accursed disease, which was a nationwide scourge during the forties and fifties. At the time she was serving with the ATS, the women's army, and stationed locally at the "Ack-Ack" (Anti-aircraft) battery in Lower Penarth, which is now part of the Glamorgan Golf Course.

She was immediately discharged from the army ("invalided out") and sent to the Sanitorium in Denbigh, North Wales, where she remained for several years until transfer to St Mary's Hospital and finally to Sully Hospital where she was operated on and only discharged after a total of nearly twelve years in hospitals.

At such a distance and during wartime travelling conditions, plus the difficulties of journeys between South and North Wales (have things changed much?), we could manage to visit poor "E" only once a month. This was, of course, the case for all other relatives of Denbigh patients, living in South Wales. So a monthly coach trip was organised, meeting in front of Cardiff Castle at about 4 a.m. on the first Sunday of each month. Probably, I was spared the ordeal of the marathon journey on many occasions, but I know that dear Mam accompanied usually by Pop undertook this regularly to give support and comfort to my sister.

With its half-asleep and dozing-off contingent of relatives, the coach would rumble off into the darkness northwards, its half-shaded headlamps barely illuminating the hedgerows of the little-more-than-lanes forming the tortuous route to Denbigh. Travelling at little more than thirty miles per hour, this monthly marathon took about seven and a half hours to reach the town of Denbigh.

There, about midday, we firstly went for lunch in a pub where Pop would call in his kindly bluff voice, laden with Somerset brogue, "I'd like a nice pot of tea !" Pop was not T.T. (tea-total) by conviction but had once seen a brewery worker in Cardiff spit into a vat and swore never to drink beer ever again.

At two we visited Enid in the Common Room of the Sanitorium, where we, the visitors, and our loved ones sat and chatted, maybe looked at the home-made gifts and foodstuffs from Mams' kitchens. A few children like me, might try our best to show off our progress at piano lessons by stumbling over the keys while our Mams glowed with pride and sisters smiled wanly their approval but pensively thought of what they were missing back at home. Their relief was all too obvious when our mutually embarrassing clumsy attempts at juvenile virtuosity were at last interrupted by some real pianist taking over the piano and livening up the rest of the afternoon with happier and unrestrained pop and rag-time melodies.

At this juncture the buzz of hurried conversations resumed, only to slow down to awkward pauses as the hands of the common room clock moved inexorably towards four o'clock, the parting bell.

Tears were shed, mostly by the Mams, maybe sighs of relief breathed surreptitiously by Dads, openly by restless kids. One can only guess at the hidden emotions of our dear ones, constrained to live apart in their Denbigh isolated community.

After another exhausting return journey southwards, we eventually got back to old Cardiff Castle at the midnight hour. How we got back to our Penarth home, I can't remember but possibly some relatively wealthy customer owning a car may have helped us. Taxis then were unthinkable for the likes of us!

Another month would pass, with letters and postcards exchanged, before the next Dawn Patrol.

Our Dear Mum

(Sorry Mum. I can't ever get the feature quite right. Clothing feature.)

Some Notable Penarth Women

1934 –

(As seen by Little Wickley Ford and also by many others)

W.H.F. 11.7.95

Miss Green
Penarth
Electrician

Mrs Hands
Landlady
(Windsor Terrace)

EVERSLEIGH GUEST HOUSE

Mrs Warren
Wise Friend

Mrs Peggy Toye (to those in need,
1st Post-Woman) All knowing on

46

SOME NOTABLE PENARTH WOMEN (1934 -)

As in every community, Penarth has had throughout its existence some women who are truly memorable for their contribution to the life of the town and/or service to others. Of these, it is usually the case that only the activities of the more prominent by reason of their high social standing on the local scene which are recorded and rewarded.

But there are always the "unsung heroes" in our midst who work quietly away with their selfless lives, neither expecting nor receiving plaudits, accolades or honours in sovereign's New Year's or Birthday Lists or anywhere else except the gratitude of those, usually poorer folk, they have helped in some way. Even from the latter they neither crave nor encourage visible recognition or celebrity.

I venture to nominate my own short list of just some of Penarth's unsung women heroes of former times:

Mrs Hands, Landlady of "Eversleigh", Guest House, Windsor Terrace.
This fine lady, whom I used to call on with Pop, on Saturday's round was a most sympathetic sponsor of Pop and constant support of our family in times of need and tragedy. For my calls for her Saturday order, led to the vestibule waiting room by the maidservant where I sat in splendour opposite the conservatory with its Victorian atmosphere of ubiquitous aspidistras and gazed with fascination at the old oil paintings of views of St Augustine's Church from the Southern orchard covered slopes surmounted by an arriving horse drawn carriage, until the grand old lady came to chat, question politely and with great interest to hear of my progress at school and concern for our family, usually ending with not only a large order but some tea and cake and a tip for me. A substantial bequest to her maidservant was typical of her.

Miss Green, Penarth's first woman electrician, who lived next door to Mrs Hands.
Miss Green was a most unusual woman for the age in that she was in advance of her time, understanding that (to most of us) relatively new phenomenon: "electricity", and in her long brown dust-coat and her large beret was often to be seen cycling around the town on her tall upright bike, with its rear mounted carrier box in which she carried home the "wet-accumulators" to re-charge and without which our wirelesses would not work. She too was a regular customer on our Saturday Round and a great friend of Mrs Hands.

Our Dear Mam
Obviously for me and my family - our greatest heroine. Her deeds and character are recorded elsewhere.

Miss Peggy Toye, John Street. Penarth's First Woman Postlady.
Still well known and respected in the town, besides being one of my first piano teachers and later being pianist for the Penarth OAPs, leading their sing-songs "down memory lane" she finally became Penarth's first post-delivery lady and became even more widely known for her spirit and cheeriness. Even in her nineties she still has that indomitable strength which continues to make her memorable.

Mrs Warren of Albert Road. Unpaid Community Social Worker and Counsellor.
Without doubt the most notable "unsung heroine" of all. She was the custodian of all practical wisdom and source of support for countless needy and desperate people in the North end of Penarth. Her husband had been one of the last drivers of the horse drawn buses between Penarth and Cardiff. Mrs Warren helped my and many other families survive all difficulties. For those, who had been threatened by the Water Company that their supply would be cut off because of an unpaid bill, she advised that this would be illegal if there were a sick person in the house. When I once fell ill and "the water man came" to do this, he went away again but only having demanded to see me and had done so. Mrs Warren WAS the Citizen's Advice Bureau of the day. Whenever Pop did not have the money to buy fruit and veg for his Saturday Round, Mrs Warren came to the rescue with a £5 loan (interest free) to be paid back on Sat. eve. She also organised a shilling a week savings club for local housewives, with a £1 payout every 20 weeks. Mrs Warren WAS the Credit Union of the day. Even amongst small children she was a much loved visitor. On his death-bed, I was told, little brother Ritchie - being distracted with fairy tales and tales of baby animals, was promised one of a clutch of newly hatched ducklings, whispered "and a duckling for Warren!"

The Aunts
and The Corner Shop. ("FORDS")

Salop Place

Aunt Alice

Aunt Grace

and Uncle Joe (26)
("Saturday Night "Returns"

© MS
March 07

48

THE AUNTS AND THE CORNER SHOP

Corner shops in "those days" were always bustling centres of local commerce, often "open all hours", but closed in typical Welsh Sunday style on that and Xmas Day. Small family businesses, they catered for just about every need, except for "booze" which was the preserve of the "off-license" (also closed on Sundays). Ragged trousered kids lingered over the big sweet bottles, trays of packeted sherbert and bootlace strings of liquorice, pondering on which to squander their half-pennies or else on a giant gobstopper of an aniseed ball. Hair curlered and beturbanned pinnied housewives queued for their weekly rations, books at the ready for the coupons to be cut out and closely eye the scales to see they got "fair shares".

Aunt Grace, large and smiling - a comfortable "body" with amiable welcome - would bring into the shop her home cooked beetroot or large platter on which reclined a succulent shoulder of ham, cooked "on the bone". No coverings protected these but fly swats and sticky flypapers were everywhere on guard.

Meanwhile sour faced Aunt Alice, thwarted in love, sparingly weighed out into dark blue paper bags quantities of sugar, which she then deftly closed, folding the tops inside one another. With a strange affinity with the vinegar, she seemed to enjoy decanting this from its cask into whichever bottle the customer had brought, but not before using a calibrated measuring jug to cost it correctly.

For their shop supplies, other than those regularly delivered in quantity by lorry, they used Pop, their brother and my father, as their buyer. He also supplied them with fish, rabbits and sometimes poultry and, of course, all their fruit and veg. But there were great disadvantages for us at No 26.

One must remember that Refrigeration of Foodstuffs, particularly in small corner shops was unknown. Even in the living quarters of "Fords' Shop", there was only a "larder" with a "cold slab" to keep perishables as long as possible. The "slab" was usually a shelf of heavy slate or marble in the coolest part of the larder which was also the coolest room in the house.

The goods that Pop supplied them with were on a "sale or return basis" and Sunday being a "closed" day all unsold perishables were sent back or rather carried back and left on our doorstep by Uncle Joe late on Saturday evening. Uncle Joe was the estranged husband of Aunt Alice and had his own single room above the shop.

And so "the Saturday night returns" became a regular mixed blessing. We needed the money! Mam and Pop struggled to make ends meet, even with the regular loans from Mrs Warren. No holidays together, no Extravagances, Clothing saved for with the "Tally Man" and his "Premier Clothing Cheques", "Make do and mend" were all the order of the day.

BUT Mam was a marvellous cook. She had learned a lot during her work "in service" in a large wealthy household in Penarth, even if she had had to leave home in Llanhilleth at the age of thirteen.

And so, although "as poor as church mice" we ate like kings! And Mam was always Queen of all!

The Captive Balloon
"......"

© Mott
2007

.... 1944

"BULLA" AND THE BARRAGE BALLOON

"Bulla" was a constant companion now and many were the doors he helped open for me. I suppose the sight of a curly haired "blondie" child, cradling a small wriggling puppy dog must have been quite appealing to the servicemen, including "the yanks" in town. In fact, even my school-mates recognized this factor and I was a welcome accomplice in waylaying these "GIs" as they visited the servicemen's NAAFI in the basement of the Albert Road Methodist Church, by way of the side lane entrance off Albert Road. There we would congregate and yell out the customary "Any Gum, Chum?" with considerable success. We were even invited inside once and Bulla and I were a great hit.

But other times, my "friends" just forgot this use for Bulla and one such time was after going "down the dock beach" to look at the tethered captive Barrage Balloon stationed on the wide space outside the Old Custom House Building (now the site of a roundabout surmounted by a bronze sculpture of a flying mermaid). Bulla was most suspicious and barked furiously at this enormous mammoth-like beast as it swayed and tugged on its mooring ropes while airmen chatted around the lorry-winch.

Tiring of my dog's barking one of the lads idly picked up a loose pebble and threw it just a few yards into the mud just off the beach. Bulla gave chase, but had to leap clear of the mud back to shore. This proved to be too much of a game for the others to resist and they quickly took it up, throwing stones further and further and further out into the glistening grey mud flats, left by the ebbing tide.

I nearly wept with horror at seeing Bulla narrowly being sucked down into the mud, but miraculously leaping free at each last moment to "plop" into another patch of mud.

At last the lads tired of the spectacle and "Bulla" answered my calls and thickly caked with the clinging mud, we slunk home to "The Terrace".

Luckily my sisters were out and Mam was able to fetch buckets of water and swill off the mud in the basement courtyard, before Bulla was allowed in to dry off in front of the fire.

That evening my sisters did take notice of him for once, but just to comment admiringly how beautifully glossy Bulla's coat was. I grinned with Mam, but we kept our secret of the powers that lie in Penarth, mud!

"Bullet", the dog
gets run
over".
Early Spring 1945.

© 8.3.07.

82.

BULLA GETS RUN OVER

We had almost finished the Saturday Round. Outside Mrs Warren's, just opposite the bottom of Belle Vue Bowling Green, I stood on the pavement and chatted to Mr Warren, as usual exchanging for one sixpence each the matchboxes I had filled with cigarette-end tobacco for his pipe. It was still war-time and pipe tobacco in short supply, so no questions asked about the origins of the "baccy".. ash trays? gutters? Meanwhile Mrs Warren stood alongside Pop at the end of the cart, waiting for him to finish weighing out her Saturday fruit and vegetables.

Just over the hill of Albert Road the road led downwards towards O'Neale's Woods and the Docks. And in the woods was an American Army Camp so big American lorries were a familiar sight and sound to us all. And so, probably by reason of this familiarity, we took little notice of the approaching low rumbling drone of such a vehicle and were shocked to hear a sudden squeal of brakes and that of an animal in pain...BULLA! He had been ambling after Pop into the roadway and had been hit by the lorry's front nearside wheel. In fact he still lay there, wriggling and squealing. But the driver, perhaps shocked, seemed unaware that the dog still lay pinned down under the front wheel.

It took seemingly ages before he understood Pop's frantic shouting and Mr Warren's gesticulations and reversed his lorry to release poor Bulla.

Then the scene transformed itself instantly into almost pure farce or a scene from BBC's Children's "Candlewick Green", as Bulla leaped up and, on three legs and fourth trailing blood, streaked away up the hill of Albert Crescent closely followed by the American Sergeant, Pop, Mr Warren, myself and it seemed a cast of scores of others, a postman, schoolboys, pram-pushing mums and Uncle Tom Cobbley and all !

Over the hill went Bulla, past St Augustine's Church and through the open doorway of our house, No 26. One can imagine the amazement of sister Bea, in the front room quietly ironing, to receive this circus invasion of Bulla and his retinue ! At last he was cornered and his leg bandaged and put in plaster.

Then followed weeks of further entertainment or rather growing impatience and irritation for me. Bulla had decided to try out his thespian skills. I was entrusted with Bulla's care and convalescence. Taking him for walks, I received all sorts of contradictory advice and reprimands. If I carried him, I was accused of being a stupid boy. "How can you expect him to get better if you don't let him exercise?" So, putting him down to walk on his own, an angry adult would accuse me of being "cruel", cautioning me that I must carry him. In an instant, Bulla would change from a snarling beast when any uniformed man passed into a pathetic mistreated puppy if any over-sympathetic lady sighed over his plight. He hammed it up for all it was worth.

It wasn't until I heard from our teacher the Aesop's fable, "Taking the Donkey to Market" that I realised how I should treat this new chameleon of a cur and Bulla finally gave up the acting profession!

FRIDAYS – 4 p.m.
"Hometime" in
Albert Road.
1940s.

"HOMETIME" in Albert Road — 1940s Fridays at 4 p.m.

"Hometime" on Frdays at 4 p.m. meant "hometime" for everyone, it seemed.

Albert Road Elementary Schools, of course finished at that time and the kids came pouring out, whooping at the freedoms to come. Infants, Senior Boys from the Upper Yard Gate, Senior Girls from the Lower Gate.

I would always run down the hill to meet my sister Bea, emerging with her cloth-covered shopping basket from which wafted the mouth watering smells of what she had cooked that afternoon and, if it evaded my clutches, would provide our tea.

The girls lower front yard presents a rural cottage-garden like tranquility on other days. Even on Fridays "at hometime" a few girls might linger awhile to sit on the tree seat and chat or wait for someone. But out on the road comes the rumble of the returning council steam roller and all the horse drawn "dust-carts" toiling slowly homewards to the council yard behind the Council Offices. Even through the windows of these Offices, one might see the staff clearing away ready for the weekend — although here my memory may have failed me as the "five day week" was not to arrive for a few decades yet and the now traditional Local Government "Poets Day" (FRIDAYS = "PUSH OFF EARLY — TOMORROW'S SATURDAY") was not even a reckless fantasy in the befuddled brain of a miserable, Clerk, General Duties.

The Firemen polish their gleaming red Fire-engine, waiting for the fire-hose to finish drying off on the railings of Belle Vue Park opposite, before they can be rolled up and replaced in their lockers on the fire-appliance.

Behind the top gate to the park, in Belle Vue Terrace, a few children play hide and seek, using the horizontally spreading evergreen bush as a den. (There has been such a bush there from time immemorial) and perhaps an anxious couple are searching for their lost cat, while two grinning mischievous urchins prepare a saucer of milk to revive the puss, which evidently has used up its ninth life!

HAPPY DAYS! But Fridays always are!

For the sake of those men, mechanical whiz kids, who frown at my sketch of "the steam roller", yes, I admit it does look a bit unusual but without the advantages of a modern overhead flange whisker and Sprocket double condenser, the manufacturer's embossed plate should give you a clue as to its highly sophisticated origins of precision engineering at its most brilliant. (Dream on, Walter Mitty !) Sketch. The knowledgeable will, of course, immediately recognize the use of the unmistakeable differential scale, the "Obergurgenheimlischenplattdeutschinselnummerrischen (u.s.w.) Format", now universally accepted (except in Dinas Powys) Here, this has led to the foreshortening of Belle Vue Park's railings to bring the top entrance and the ever popular kids' den into the picture.

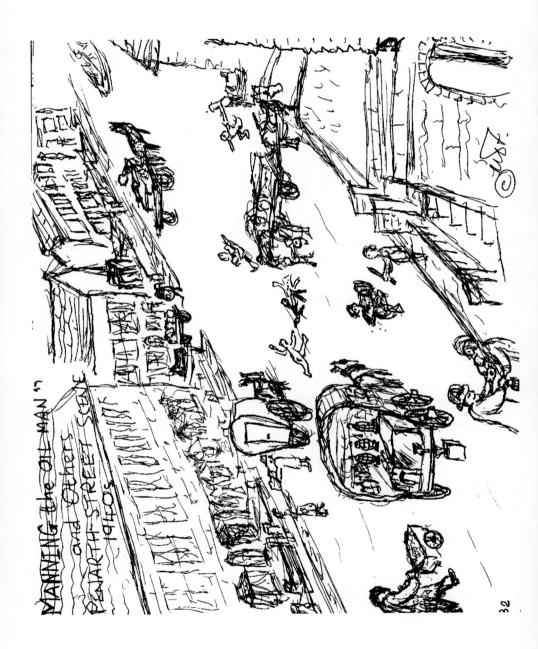

MANNING the OIL MAN "S and Others PENARTH STREET SCENE 1940s

56

"MANNING, THE OIL MAN" (and others) - STREET SCENE, 1940s

"Pictures in the mind" can stay with us all our lives, refresh us and enliven our hours of solitude in later life. For me, the visual images of the bustling activity of the street scenes of my childhood always evoke the sounds, smells and sights of the huge variety of horse drawn traffic around Penarth.

Oh, Yes, certainly the realization that the Internal Combustion Engine had come to stay was reinforced by the increasing number of cars and lorries everywhere. And I will always remember the later terrifying, nerve-jangling excitement of being taken by newly demobbed Mr Davis, his spouse and the twins back with them to Maidenhead in their new Ford car. 60 m.p.h. seemed just about super-sonic to us three boys in the back, and we craned our necks to verify our speed on the glisteningly new speedo dial in front of Mr Davis, the needle going as far as it could!

But horses still ruled the roads. Maybe never all on the same day, as I have sketched, but Pembroke Terrace had regular visits from "Manning, The Oil Man" and many others with their work animals.

MR MANNING lived in Ludlow Street, just down from the corner where the original Robert James kept his ironmongery shop. Even then his was the most memorable of all the horse-drawn vehicles. It resembled an American pioneer's covered wagon battling overland, bringing civilization to the West. But here in Penarth it was just Albert Road Hill it had to conquer as it travelled North ! With its, if fine, rolled up canvas sides revealing the huge paraffin tank inside and its new oil lamps, saucepans, swinging from the side bars and other household goods stashed inside it made its round of the households to bring the means of light, heat and other creature comforts to those of us still not "connected".

HOLTOM'S BREAD VAN. This tall, elegant large wheeled enclosed van resembled one of the old Bow Street Runners' Prisoner transports but certainly kept the bread fresh and clean for us.

PREMIER COAL COMPANY. Mr Best lived in Bradfield Place but also had coal sidings at Penarth Railway Station with offices in part of what is now the Glendale Restaurant, just opposite.

THE SALT SELLERS (NO, NOT CELLARS!) From time to time, this cart, bearing huge blocks of salt would appear and men would sit astride these to saw off a chunk for you.

RAG AND BONE MAN. Using all the clever sales psychology of that era, this itinerant wanderer of Penarth's streets and lanes, yodling "Eh= EE= Owe= Ine" or "RAG-BOH !" was pre-armed with either an assortment of colourful balloons or else a tank of goldfish and ready supply of cheap glass bowls. Kids would rush out from all directions and many a Mam would lose their lineful of washing and Dad more than just his shirt on a Saturday!

BESIDES HORSES and carts, came the Knife Grinder with his adaptable bike and The Pikelet Man! The latter clumped around North Penarth, pushing his home made cart – a box on pram wheels, laden with hot pikelets, protected by an old sack.

Whenever I see period films like "Oliver", or "Shakespeare in Love", I always think that all that was needed to further enliven our street scenes and create a full scenario was a Nell Gwyn, inviting us kids "won't you buy my juicy oranges?" But everyday was a free spectacle for us!

58

THE STABLE IN WINDSOR TERRACE LANE

Pop's stable in Windsor Terrace Lane occupied about half of Mrs Maisie's back garden in Windsor Terrace itself. It was, in my day, a ramshackle edifice, roughly built of concrete blocks and overhung with sheets of rusting corrugated iron which covered not only the long stable itself but extended further to cover the narrow walkway between the horse's entrance but also the small storage area bounded by the neighboring garden wall and the boundary wall before Windsor Lane.

The cart with its long shafts, rested in the open area alongside the stable.

The storage area was a veritable "curiosity shop" for a child such as me. In it lay stacked haphazardly the thrown-out objects from house sales for which Pop had been employed as a carter. Various pieces of furniture but also pictures, Chinese puzzle boxes, and books, mouldering away but often of antiquarian interest. But the Antique trade was nowhere as universally popular as TV programmes, car boot sales and the consumerism of nostalgia have made it nowadays. To my great regret, I realize that this detritus of old Victorian households in Penarth would today have been of enormous interest, if not value.

The poor old horse, stabled in the dark if dry fetid atmosphere of its cave-like shelter, just lay and slept on its bed of straw and wood shavings or stood with its head poking out above the half-door, looking for food or water, for which a bucket stood ready nearby.

From nails hammered into the cross-beam of the roof supports hung drying rabbit skins, for which Pop could get perhaps a few shillings from glove-makers or their agents in Cardiff.

But, if an opportunity came for me to spend any time combing through all the bric-a-brac, I would often find an old picture post-card album filled with memorabilia from an even earlier age…. filigreed St. Valentine Cards, highly ornate Christmas Cards, Greetings Cards from some rich Aunt in Baden-Baden or some wealthy traveller doing the obligatory Grand European Tour.

But what I was looking for were postage stamps for I had by now become a passionate stamp collector and only now do I understand my almost sacrilegious acts of vandalism in tearing off the corners of those cards bearing postage stamps and throwing away the ruined remnants.

Some too bulky items of furniture also passed through our household, given to Pop as unsaleable after house auctions. One such piece was a magnificent mahogany Captain's dining table which, with its spare extra leaves could be extended to a length of some twenty feet. This stayed with us for some years although we never had room to extend it fully.

In the late fifties my sister Enid, now owner of the house and wishing to dispose of this table and possibly having a mahogany bookcase made from its materials, accepted the offer from a Pontypridd Woodwork teacher to dismantle it, take away the timber and make such a bookcase for her, only keeping any wood left over as payment.

In retrospect, it was another act of vandalism to take apart this marvellously crafted, skilfully jointed and expertly engineered extending masterpiece. It took the teacher, my brother and myself almost a whole day to disassemble it, load his car until it was groaning with the weight and watch it slowly disappear at the end of the road. Neither the teacher, nor a mahogany bookcase were ever seen again!

But perhaps the magic of the stable was still working and this was all illusion, after all!

"HARNESSING AND HARVESTING"
WINDSOR TERRACE LANE — SUMMER 1944

© NDT.
B2

60

HARNESSING AND HARVESTING

Out from the stable in Windsor Terrace Lane, we would firstly drag the cart to the opposite side of the lane and position it by the side of Mr Guidi's long orchard-garden. It would always be an early morning of a Saturday as this was the day of The Round and firstly we would have to get to Cardiff and back before starting.

Overhanging the lane, apples and pears would hang in profusion from the orchard and Pop, knowing that quite often these would either never be picked and simply rot or else be roughly "harvested" by gangs of marauding urchins armed with sticks or stones to try to bring down the damaged or inedible fruit, would get me to climb up onto a box perched on the empty cart and harvest for him. Pop hated to see waste!

Meanwhile he would go back inside to bring out the horse. With its collar inverted to get it over its head, the headband secured with its blinkers, metal bit and halter in place, Pop would back the horse in between the shafts, link up the traces, secure the saddle, the belly band and all other parts of the harness and we were ready.

Climbing up with me onto the cart, Pop would smile at our harvest of fruit and together we would set off for market.

I cannot say for sure what happened to the fruit. We must have benefited somehow and times were hard.

Worse things happened in those days and I cannot believe that kind benign old Mr Guidi, owner of the popular ice cream parlour in Stanwell Road, near the town-centre roundabout would have begrudged the extra fruit or even suffered as a result. To appease my conscience, I often ask myself, "Of all these most respectable and upright citizens I see on the streets of my hometown, how many of them can truthfully say that, as children they never, ever, scrumped for apples?"

Six pence
for Comics

SIXPENCE FOR COMICS

Being the youngest child and, of course the youngest son, I suppose I was always over-indulged. My every interest was catered for. My great interest in words, greatly enriched by the ever present conversation of adults who always included me in their chat, plus the availability of mountains of books, left –overs from house auctions and given to Pop when houses were finally cleared meant that I was never short of reading material.

But every child loved comics. Old second-hand shops, as the one at the top end of Glebe Street, had piles of dog-eared, often tatty and not too clean old ones for sale. And the variety was enormous as was the age-range catered for. From "Tiny Tim" and such like for toddlers and infants, through "Beano" and "Dandy", to "Film Fun" for addicts of Laurel and Hardy and Charlie Chaplin, and other favourite film comedians to ""Hotspur" and the like for fairly fluent readers who didn't need so many pictures and had graduated from comic strip type comics. For more affluent children from middle-class homes "The Boy's Own Paper" and Arthur Mees' "Children's Newspaper" were the top of the range. But even copies of some of these sometimes filtered down to be found occasionally amongst the second-hand shop dross.

For me however, Saturdays held the high spot of the week. Not only the adventures of our fascinating weekly sorties to Cardiff's Central Market, the bustling trade of Custom House Street and the whole subsequent day, but the actual last stage of our journey into town was eagerly anticipated with great relish.

As the horse, with a lightly laden cart behind it trotted along towards the start of St Mary Street to enter the darkness under the railway bridge, Pop would press a bright silver sixpence into the palm of my hand and quietly mutter, smiling the while, "Well, off you go ! ...wait for you the other side !"

I needed no further urging, but slipped down from the cart and ran.

In the wide doorway of the big hotel on the corner, with its crazy-paving-like stone facade and its arched windows, always sat the Newspaper Vendor with all the newspapers laid out as were the comics. I made my choice, which over the years became more selective and mature, handed over the coin and ran to catch up with Pop.

Even during that morning, while "holding the horse's head" and waiting for Pop outside the market or in Custom House Street I would riff through them, but look forward pleasurably to bedtime when, by torchlight under the bedclothes, I would read and read....earlier, of Desperate Dan and Lord Snooty and Dennis the Menace......and, as my reading got better, of Wilson the Miracle Athlete, of Cannon Ball Kid and on and on until I fell asleep and Mam, checking on me, took away the still shining torch.

Yes, Sixpence for Comics was a lot of money in those days, but the delights of reading were priceless.

"Charity begins......"

"CHARITY BEGINS AT HOME"

Pop was always quietly on the look-out for those he thought less fortunate than himself. His modest soft hearted and unselfish acts of charity went largely unnoticed, which was the way he obviously wanted it. However one day a nun, a rare sight on the streets of Penarth, came knocking on all the doors of our street, Pembroke Terrace, collecting for charity. As Mam opened the front door, the nun caught a glimpse of Pop moving about busily way back at the end of the corridor. In her soft Irish voice, the nun exclaimed: "Ahhr, so this is where Mr Forrr.d lives, is it?" Having been given something by Mam, she quietly went on to the next house.

Often as a child accompanying Pop to Cardiff- perhaps .to Custom House Street and the noisily bustling warren of streets around there, full of horses and carts, a few lorries, and dark caverns with their haphazardly piled crates and sacks, filled with fruit or vegetables and the whispered haggling of the dealers and small traders or else a much relished visit to Cardiff market with its bright lights, merry stallholders and delicious smells of mouth watering foods, Pop would notice some desolate wretch of a beggar.

Passing a few paces further he would quietly stop, turn and unobtrusively grasp my hand and press into it a half-crown, a not inconsiderable sum for him in those days. Then he would point back to the perhaps physical wreck of a beggar and whisper, "Go and put that into his cap!" At first I would be too embarrassed to do so, but from the very first occasion this happened, Pop would be quietly insistent and slowly I learned from him his way of charity. Later in life, I came across the lines, which seemed to epitomize Pop's valuable lessons:

"Do good by stealth, and blush to find it fame"

No Hancock he, with that overblown comedic act, boasting of how the very lapels of his jackets were so full of holes from the vast number of charity flags he had bought and worn., that his coat was almost falling apart

What we had we, as a family, shared. We still remember with affection the penniless Indian student he met in a Cardiff Street.

He was invited by Pop to come and stay with us – which he did for about a year. Pop then found out that the student didn't have the daily bus fare to Cardiff, so promptly gave him this regularly. In common with many others in this "poorer" area of the town, the legacies of our parents' examples were riches indeed.

82.

Saturdays (dawn start)
To market. To market.
(The War Years
(39-45)

"Examining Gin Traps and Snares -
Penarth Road (below Llandcoog)"

"Picking up produce from Allotment
by R. Ely.

TERRY ROCHE

EDWA

"Buying More in
Wholesale Fruit and Veg Market (pre-Bessant)"

A welcome
snack in
Cardiff Central ©
Market 2007 ASW

"TO MARKET, TO MARKET" The War Years, 1939 – 45

Saturdays were always the busiest.

It was the Day for "The Round".... "The Saturday Round", when with fully laden cart, I used to go with Pop all around Penarth to all our regular customers to serve them at their front doors with all they needed in the way of fruit and veg, sometimes rabbits, if Pop had managed to catch any, and sometimes a chicken or fish, if he had any left from Friday.

But first, up very early, perhaps 5 a.m. and after a quick mug of hot strong tea, sweetened with treacle (coz it wasn't on ration like sugar) and a "rough doorstep" of bread and marge, again with treacle, we'd be off to the stable in Windsor Terrace Lane.

Once on the road, it took us quite some time before we'd eventually get to Market. First we had to stop in Penarth Road, just below the small reservoir for Llandough for Pop to check on his snares or gin traps. Then on to the allotment to collect what we'd picked or dug the day before , then stop for a second bite to eat at the tin shack just by Grangetown Railway Station Bridge. If it was a cold winter's day and I had been sheltering against frost or rain under old potato sacks, I'd be glad to huddle there with the lorry drivers in the warm fug for a few minutes.

Then on to Cardiff Central Market to sell some stall-holders our produce in season: radishes, lettuces, blackcurrants, red currants, goosegogs, carrots and if lucky maybe a sack of horseradish-roots Pop had managed to find somewhere.

What came next was my greatest treat. ....a Snack at Roche's at the end of the market nearest St John's church. I can still taste the sweet succulence of his brawn sandwiches and the hot sweet tea to wash 'em down with.

But next came the main business....to Custom House Street, where all the bustling coming and going and to-ing and fro-ing was really exciting. I had to "hold the horse's head" while Pop went off to buy things we couldn't grow like oranges, bananas and all that kind of stuff.. While I waited, I'd breathe in the lovely warm soggy Weatabix-like smell in the air. Only later did I learn that it was the smell of the nearby Brewery.

Usually Pop would call me over and I'd be very proud helping him with a deal: "If there are a gross of oranges in this case, Mickey and they want two pounds for them,. how much will I have to charge for each one to make a profit ?" It was just like Mental 'Rith back at school. but much more fun. I felt quite grown up when I helped out like that.

We usually got back home at about half past nine. There'd be a lovely smell wafting up the outside stone steps from Mam's cooking. Sometimes there'd be lorry drivers from Robert England's or William Bradnum's, sitting down to bacon and eggs with us too.... well we couldn't eat with them looking on, could we ?

By now it was probably about quarter past ten, but our day had just begun. Finish loading the cart and, with any luck we'd be home for tea by six o'clock, stable the horse and sit down by the wireless to listen to Saturday Night at the Hippodrome.

Pop would count the money and change all my tips: one penny for each half penny I had.

We'd talk just before bed about where Pop and I would go the following day, Sunday..

Perhaps to The Funfair at Barry, or Cold Knap Lake or even down to Llantwit Major, past the RAF place (to see any planes we could from the top of the double-decker bus) and walk down to the beach there... although you couldn't go on it because of the barbed wire there.

It had been a great day, although sometimes I'd listen to the other kids talking about playing footie on Saturdays, but I didn't have time for that, did I? One day, one day...

"Getting ready for the Saturday Round." (1945)

"Now last of all, The weights and scales.

GETTING READY FOR THE SATURDAY ROUND

Having arrived back at No 26 from our early morning trip to Cardiff and having finished our third (?) breakfast, it was time to get the cart ready.

Already on the cart was the fresh produce we had collected from the Penarth Road smallholding, in season soft fruit, radishes, salads, rhubarb, artichokes, spinach, cabbage and whatever else plus those things we had managed to get in Custom House Street from the wholesale stores there. Occasionally, sometimes as a special treat at Christmas there might have been a shipment of oranges or bananas and even then it depended on the good will of the particular vendors and if the larger greengrocery shops had not grabbed the lot, we might have some exotic fruit for our regulars.

There had been a heated argument once when a housewife from just around the corner, coming back from town with her basket already laden with fruit and veg, had spotted the Fyffes Banana box on the cart and had demanded some for herself. But the "regulars" crowding around the cart had soon seen her off even though it had shaken Pop with her threat to "report him". But it was war-time and common-sense usually prevailed, Traders could reasonably be allowed to use this even with unrationed goods.

Anyway, here stood the half laden cart and time was pressing. Sacks and boxes waiting in the scullery had to be carried through the house, up the stone steps to the street and loaded. After a while, I started to take an interest in how. Why load the everyday necessities, the basics, "the staples", like potatoes, carrots, onions and cabbage on the "nearside" the pavement side of the cart, when all these would be bought anyway ? And so making an attractive display of the more expensive items, the occasional exotic and home grown fruits in season plus the Xmas specials on this side of the cart became a weekly challenge. Here, hopefully, the eyes of any housewife standing waiting on the pavement by the cart or even a passer-by might be tempted and force them to open a purse even wider.

Then the boxes had to be broken open ready. Pop had once cut himself badly on a protruding nail or jagged piece of broken box-wood, so I made it my business to open all boxes wide and hammer in all exposed nails.

Lastly, and most importantly, the weights and scales. These had to be checked and officially lead-sealed annually by the Government Inspector and I usually helped Pop carry these down to the basement of Plassey Street Tabernacle Church for this examination and approval. I knew by now that with our 14, 7, 2, 1, half, quarter pound and 2 and 1 ounce weights we could make all the necessary combinations.

After a final drink of tea, we were off !

Just then I reminded Pop, "Remember that we must get to The Rectory in Hickman Road about 1 o'clock. The lady there said she needed some manure for her roses!"

Pop nodded amiably. He knew the keen gardeners on his round and since the horse was of regular bodily function, it would always oblige at about that hour and the route of the round varied from time to time to please these particular customers in turn, always ready and waiting with their shovels and buckets at about 1 o'clock!

FOOL WEATHER DAYS

70

FOUL WEATHER DAYS

Most people of my generation, i.e. children during WW2, seem to remember mostly the weather then as almost permanent sunshine and balmy playtime evenings which were endless. Maybe this was because of the wartime government decision to enact "Double Summertime", which would help the war effort. But probably for those children like myself, whose fathers worked on the land or outside throughout the year, harsher foul weather is also memorable.

Winters could be cruel and summer rainstorms left us sodden and miserable with no chance of drying off in a centrally heated house.

The fabled rhymes of infancy had real meaning and relevance to us still:
"Watch out, watch out, Jack Frost is about, He's after your fingers and toes" reminded us of chilblains and frozen fingers. Our Mums threaded through our coat sleeves the elastic which held our woollen gloves in place, ever ready to protect us, and:

"Greasy Joan doth keel the pot" was the reality still as many households had simply a cold tap for water, (unless one had a water heating geyser in the kitchen.) And cold linoleum greeted your morning waking feet as you rushed from your icy bedroom downstairs to where, hopefully, Dad had already lit the coal fire with newspaper and split logs prepared the night before. The reassuring sound of roaring as he held a spread newspaper sheet over the burgeoning infant fire to create an updraft and "draw" the fire, signalled that Dad was already up about his business.

For Pop and me, the weather on Saturdays was particularly important. Saturdays were the days of "The Round" with horse and cart around the town with no shelter from the elements. Yes, old potato sacks, shielded me from the numbing frost on our cart journey to Cardiff and Custom House Street at 5.30 a.m., but if the rain, sleet or snow caught us later, "On The Round", we just had to get on with it.

Just occasionally, Pop would turn the horse homeward for a brief warming. Then Dear Mum would be ready with just a small tot of brandy for him and a hot drink for me, to fortify us to go back out again for the rest of that Saturday.

"And miles to go before we sleep."

"Bookworm on Wheels"

Summer 1963 — Approaching Whitchurch Village

© MD?

BOOKWORM ON WHEELS

Always on the lookout for ways of earning the extra money to keep his family afloat, Pop would offer his services, as often as he could get the work, as a carter. Usually an estate agent would offer him work and invite him to a house sale or auction, at the end of which buyers from near and far would be looking for someone with transport, such as a horse and cart, to take their purchases home for them.

Along with the fine furniture from some of the larger houses in Penarth, the house clearance meant that there were often piles of old books. Sometimes these were wanted, sometimes not by the person employing Pop and his horse and cart. And very often I went with Pop, to help carry in the smaller items.

If I was lucky there might be children's books amongst the left-overs and I would be allowed to keep these. But whatever kind of books they were, I always enjoyed the long slow journeys which would take at least a couple of hours to reach the furthermost parts of Cardiff or beyond.

If it were fine and no need for a protective tarpaulin, I could usually find somewhere comfortable to sit on the cart until journey's end and become engrossed in the contents of some book of adventure stories and oblivious to the traffic or the people we passed. I became more and more addicted to the reading habit, a veritable "book worm" in fact.

The only downside of my reading was that some of the books, already antiquated, often contained Encyclopaedic "facts" in the sciences, which had already been either disproved or overtaken by more modern research and so, typically, I became more of a dreamer than ever and tended more and more to indulge in romantic fantasies leading my studies eventually towards fiction and to be less well versed in science.

But, all the same, being a "bookworm on wheels" was a delight, particularly in summer!

Little Fauntleroy
Lord Knot Lake
Cold 1944
R.

LITTLE LORD FAUNTLEROY MICKEY

There's no doubt about it, I was a spoilt brat! The apple of my father's eye, overindulged and "spoilt".

This happened for all sorts of reasons, perhaps the fact of my being the youngest and last child, perhaps because I had escaped the worst of the years of The Great Depression, more than likely also because of the tragic deaths of my immediate two preceding siblings which led to my having been overprotected and indulged. A mixture of all these factors most likely contributed, but I benefited in many ways too.

Sundays always meant that Pop took me somewhere with him as a regular treat. I learned in later life that sister Enid had envied this free Sunday with Pop. She told me that she had sometimes asked Mam why they too couldn't come along as well. Mam smiled and explained, "We are the women. We stay at home and cook the Sunday dinner." Perhaps it was common in those days for these roles to be accepted but even then, evidently, this was being questioned by the younger generation of women.

Besides seasonal outings into the countryside around Penarth, to pick blackberries in the Autumn and primroses in Spring or just walking and looking for mushrooms in Tinkinswood or as far as Cwrt yr Rala, Pop would regularly take me to one of three destinations: to the funfair at Barry Island, to the lake at Cold Knap or by bus to Llantwit Major where, passing the RAF base at St Athans and trying to see any aeroplane taking off and wondering whether it was the same type as brother George flew, we would walk the length of the long lane down to the beach. We could never get onto the beach itself because of the barbed wire strung in huge coils as a precaution against any possible invasion.

But it was at the Funfair and even more so at Cold Knap that I really felt like the storybook character, Little Lord Fauntleroy. Without any other friends of my own age I would go on all "the rides", even the scenic railway on my own. Pop paid but just watched from afar.

Worse still, at Cold Knap, Pop would pay a boatman to row me around the ornamental lake in great style. I would always feel most self-conscious about this and suspected that the silent beady eyed boatman, perspiring away, most probably viewed me as just that: "Little Lord Fauntleroy". Thank goodness none of the other kids from school could have seen me, otherwise my life would have been even more uncomfortable of a Monday.

"'Allo, 'Allo, 'Allo"

... Mickey - the Master Criminal

"MICKEY – THE MASTER CRIMINAL"

While appreciating that Cardiff Jail, and all other jails throughout the land, are probably filled with inmates, all of whom claim to be innocent, my experience of first encounters with the long arms of the law made me nervously aware that real "innocence" is often no protection from strong feelings of guilt, even if completely unwarranted.

On then quiet St Augustine's Road, I had been again playing with Arthur – this time idly trying to improve my skills as a pedal cyclist and giving him " a lift" on my crossbar just for the short stretch of flat road outside his house, opposite "The Plantation".

Suddenly a loud deep throated bellow announced the presence of two burly policemen confronting us. Slipping off the crossbar, Arthur whistled away home like a whippet on top form.

Then followed my first police interview.

"DIDN'T YOU KNOW IT'S AGAINST THE LAW TO RIDE TWO ON A BICYCLE?"
Timorously but with complete honesty, I replied, "No, sir!"
Doubtfully, trying to be helpful (or so I thought at the time), "DID YOUR FRIEND KNOW?"
Now warming to Mr Policeman and trying to be equally helpful, "I don't know sir, but I'll go and ask him, if you like."

Abruptly changing tone, former kind Mr Policeman snarls, "DON'T BE CHEEKY!"
Young Constable comes to the rescue, "I THINK I KNOW HIM, SARGE. IT'S LITTLE MICKEY FORD, ISN'T IT?"

"SARGE" peers more closely into my quivering face. "YES, IT CERTAINLY IS. NOW THEN.... WE KNOW YOU AND (ominously) WE KNOW WHERE YOU LIVE. WE KNOW YOUR AUNT'S IN THAT CORNER SHOP AND WE'LL BE HAVING A WORD WITH THEM ABOUT YOU! RIGHT, OFF YOU GO AND JUST DON'T LET US CATCH YOU AGAIN!!!

With sighs of relief I climb the hill to Pembroke Terrace and home. Dear Pop had always been chanting a little rhyme to me ending with the couplet, "If he kicks or if he wails, take him off to Cardiff Jail!"

THIS TIME, despite my close encounter with The Law, I had at least escaped that fate. But I had been most impressed with this display of Police Intelligence. Clearly they were well informed about the backgrounds of all potential master criminals in the town, including Mickey Ford ! I would have to watch my step.

****

A few days later, innocently walking along Windsor Terrace towards the Town Centre, I became aware of the same two Police Officers earnestly walking towards me. By now scared witless by my last Police Interview, I desperately looked around for a means of avoiding them.
Seeing the invitingly open gates of The Old Rectory near Rectory Road Lane, I skidaddled inside and a few paces along the noisily scrunching gravel driveway. But......Too Late ! Behind me boomed seemingly Judge Jeffries himself, "OH YESSS! IF IT ISN'T LITTLE MICKEY FORD AGAIN! WHAT ARE YOU UP TO THIS TIME, THEN? A SPOT OF BREAKING AN' ENTERING, IS IT???"

"'Scuse me mister—
Know any foreign words?"

New Boy
and
Visiting Tutor

THE
LURE
OF
LANGUAGE(S)

— BEGINNINGS, AND

Y FENTRE

82

THE LURE OF LANGUAGE(S)

Although Mam had originally come from a Welsh speaking family in the coal mining valleys of Monmouthshire, her parents had not passed the language on to their children, using it between themselves for private family matters. She still had certain phrases, of course, and these I picked up readily enough, not even thinking about their being from a different language or culture. Penarth was predominantly English speaking, anyway, being in the south east corner of Wales and many people, including Pop's father, had migrated here from the West Country.

So it was really only with the irregular introduction of "Welsh Lessons" at school that I became more aware of differences. And with my growing passion for stamp collecting with all those strange words on the stamps and even different squiggly-looking letters that I came to realize that most fascinating of facts: that foreign people had completely different words for even familiar objects.

This was, for me, an almost magical discovery. It was almost akin to the discovery of the Rosetta Stone.

I started to try to make lists of these strange words and their meanings, asking just about every adult, "Please do you know any foreign words?" With growing amazement I found out that most did! The postman, any sailor, or soldier or airman I encountered, even the barber and the milkman were all pestered by me.. And then I discovered the old school books used by my brothers now away in the RAF. Spanish and German words and phrases were all there and I longed to learn more.

But more immediately, Welsh !

The school lessons were not very good and only rarely did the teacher hang up on the black-board and tell us the single words for the buildings and activities portrayed in the poster picture of a village, saying, "This is an "eglwys" (church). What is it ? "And we would monotonously chant after him, parrot fashion", Eglwys", and so it went on. Not very inspiring.

But then an unusual event took place. A new boy arrived in the class. He was from a bi-lingual home and the language used at home was Welsh. It was his first language. Days later, miraculously, a visiting Welsh teacher arrived as his own tutor and just sat there by his side chatting away in Welsh armed with fascinating school books in Welsh, too!

Was I envious ? Of course, and jealous too. Why couldn't I have a Welsh teacher like this?

And so the lure of languages began

I did eventually get on a one-year intensive Welsh course. But that's another story.

Music of
the Hours.
"Play it again!"

"Roll over,
Beethoven?"

MAESTEG HOUSE

PIANO
LESSONS I

PIANO LESSONS I

Even now, at age 73, I am still "learning the piano"! Slow learner, or what?

But what has intrigued me from a very early age, was not only the instrument and how to play it, but the great variety and wonderful range of teachers who have, in turn, attempted their very best to help me progress, if only for personal and private enjoyment which music making can bring.

Whether I was initially captivated and motivated to embark on this lifelong quest by the seemingly brilliant playing of my sister Bea (who typically denies ever having been any great shakes at playing) I don't know. But I do quite clearly remember sitting quietly in the bay window seat of the best "front room", diametrically opposite the corner of St Augustine's Churchyard listening, enraptured by her seemingly flawless renditions of Chopin's "Polonaises".
Anway, I was hooked. And the long journey began....with my first two piano teachers.

Miss Goodman was a very pleasant elderly lady, living just two doors away from the top yard entrance to Albert Elementary School but I don't think I lasted long with her. And the reason for termination of lessons with her was not strictly musical, but might be encapsulated in Sir John Betjeman's famous poetry anthology title, "Summoned by Bells".

For whatever reason, my weekly lessons were to be from 8.30 a.m. until 9 a.m. but Miss Goodman, in kindly but firm tone would regularly insist just about 9 a.m. that I "play it again, please!". Those readers of my first book may well remember "Town Boy or Home Boy ?" and I was still fearful of the routine interrogation of late arrivals by the Headmaster wielding his cane. The sound of the urgently ringing school handbell just a few yards away made me aware of "The Music of the Hours" and so before long I bade farewell to Miss Goodman and went on to meet my second piano teacher, with whom I was to stay for several years.

Miss Peggy Toye, who lived at one end of John Street, in Maesteg House. I believe I may well have been one of Peggy's favourites and was quite fond of her and her colourful expressions which always made the enthusiasms she engendered really memorable. Allowing her pupils free range in choice of musical pieces, I enthused about Tchaikovsky and Twelfth Street Rag as well as surprising her by "working up" on my own "Sonata Pathetique" and her delicious comment brings a sentimental smile even now. With a dreamlike expression, Peggy turned to me and said "Oh, Michael, That's a smashin' number!"

Whenever and wherever I hear Beethoven's music now, I still smile inwardly and have to agree, **"Yes, Dear Peggy, you were so right. Beethoven certainly did compose some smashin' numbers!"**

Rolling Lawn & Peaches Galore

Summer 1943

ROLLING LAWN AND PEACHES GALORE

Another occasional job for Pop was to take the horse along to the big house in Bradford Place, just below Penarth Head, and roll the lawn. This was an immense circular lawn, bounded at the far side by the cliffs, along the top of which was a long path overlooking the sea which was called "Admiral's Walk". And indeed it would have been a fine walk for any Admiral, with its panoramic view of the sea as far as Flat Holme and Steep Holme, the coast of Somerset and the ships and yachts which passed below.

To protect the lawn, firstly huge sandal-like leather shoes had to be buckled onto the horse's hoofs. Then, after loading the large wooden box surmounting the immense roller, the horse would be backed in between the shafts and Pop would begin the lengthy task of rolling the lawn from end to end, turning and walking the horse back again carefully just overlapping the previous roll. Of course the lawn had already been cut by somebody else. The whole process lasted through the afternoon

Meanwhile I would be trying to make friends with the gardener, who was picking trugs of peaches from the tall fan-trained peach trees which hugged the retaining wall of Penarth Head's park above. The trees had been trained along wires for decades it seemed, and the story went that just as it had been a Roman tradition two old carthorses had been slaughtered on the spot before the trees were planted.

But, although I was simply drooling at the sight of these luscious fruit simply dripping in abundance from the branches, the mean old gardener ignored my sighs. But the lady of the house did bring out for Pop and me a large jug of cooling freshly made lemonade.

I still remember those peaches though and it has always been my ambition to grow my own – though without benefit of any sacrificial horses!

THE (WELCOME) NIGHT VISITOR II
1943 ? 44 ?

THE (WELCOME) NIGHT VISITOR

A loud banging on the front door awakened us all. It was the middle of the night. Whoever could it be?

Sleepily I left my bedroom and followed Pop, with his flickering candle, to the front door, with Mam bleary-eyed just behind me.

For just a few seconds, we just stared at the dim figure on the doorstep, then Mam and I whooped with joy and Pop grinned his welcome. It was brother George, my own RAF pilot brother, also grinning from ear to ear.

We happily ushered him along the corridor and down the stairway to our basement front sitting room. Then, while Pop busied himself putting on the kettle next door and then trying to revive the fire from the barely live coals left in the fire cage of the old welsh fire range, Mam gazed proudly and lovingly at her second son, listening avidly to his every word.

Not leaving me out, George pushed towards me the strangely colourful woven basket, inviting me to look inside. To my delight was revealed a collection of exotic fruits, only some of which I recognized but even these I barely remembered from pre-war times.

It seemed that George had just returned from Lisbon in Portugal. He had been there with a number of other officers and warrant officers – all dressed in "mufti" (civilian clothes) as Portugal was a neutral country in the war. It was all very mysterious. Later he showed me the secret compass, hidden inside a brass button and how a magnetized propelling pencil's clasp could be balanced on the pointed tip to form another north-finder. I never did find out what "they" had been doing there.

George stayed a few days before returning to his base, but being a pilot with Transport Command and based in Britain, he managed to get home several times during the war and I got to know him quite well, whereas brother Jack – also in the RAF – was always abroad and I was not to see him for six years.

George was always sympathetic to his little brother, often played with me and took great interest in my childhood hobbies, such as stamp-collecting. For many years I treasured the plain stamp album, in which he painstakingly headed the successive pages alphabetically with the names of all the countries.

But, of all his visits, it is the memory of the surprise night visit which remains most vividly in my mind's eye.

"Listenin
to the
Radio
Winter
1943

© AWD?
8.3.07

86

LISTENING TO THE WIRELESS: 1943

An atmosphere of family bliss and harmony pervades the gas-lit basement sitting room at No 26, Pembroke Terrace, Penarth. There was me, ... me Mam and "Pop".

"Pop" - I, little Mickey Ford had dubbed him this, after frequently reading the strip cartoon by that name in the "Daily Sketch". The only resemblance between the two was the enormous belly, which my Dad, "my Pop" supported with a wide low hanging leather belt. (he also wore braces beneath his waistcoat) My Pop also differed from the other one in that the paper had theirs as a "toff"...a city gent with bowler, smart black jacket and pin-striped trousers ...and SHOES !

MY Pop wore BOOTS ....and corduroy breeches, and leggings and ...and ...well, you get the picture? Of an evening before settling down by the roaring fire to sit with Mam and listen to the wireless with Mam, he'd take off his old wrinkled tie , the soiled detachable collar, his leggings and boots before patting Bullet, my mongrel dog, on the head as he lay beside the big old armchair.

Then he'd look at the fire. If it looked sickly poor, he would get one of the drying logs or tree stumps from the hearth and shove into the midst of the coals in the fire basket of the old Welsh Fire Range and despite Mam's low mumbled warnings shove one to jam up the chimney too....we had had the fire brigade out a few times with "chimney on fire" callout. No matter, we were all safe and cosy... what if the fire did roar a bit... it just added to the warmth of love which embraced all there.

Then, once he had settled, I would climb up onto my Pop's lap to nestle there, listening as he "tuned in". I liked it especially when he laughed. "The news" always brought worried looks to the grown ups' faces and they would look at each other silently but knowingly.

But if it was "Saturday Night and Happidrome" that was different. My Pop was jolly. He laughed and even though sometimes, I didn't quite understand all the jokes, I laughed just the same.... to make Pop smile down at me and give me a "rough cuddle", rubbing his chin stubble against my cheek. We were together, we were a family in this small cosy room. The news might be bad, but here we were safe and together. The wireless did that for us. Evenings by the wireless were memorable.

The myriad of marvelous listening shut out all the other worries of the day. The panoply of memorable characters in Tommy Handley's ITMA were a tonic: Funf, the incompetent German Spy, Mrs Mop with her "Can I do yer now, Sir",: Don't forget the Diver, Colonel Chinstrap and a boozy "Don't mind if I do!" and, and.... And of course there were, oh, so many other programmes to lift the spirits in wartime.

Sir Harry Lauder was one of his favorites and he used to hum along to Sir Harry's finale, "We'll take the High Road " The accent was broad Scots and I lived it too.

The programme usually had Rob Wilton in it, and how we laughed at his long doleful monologue. I quickly learned the opening words of his act and his slow, serious delivery of his lines: "The day War broke out, my wife said to me.........." It made fun of the war and we could laugh at it for a while. All too soon, the closing cheery song ending with a farewell from "Ramsbottom, Enoch and me......" brought Mam to her feet to make us all a hot drink before bed.

Yes, despite it all, the wireless brought us together for a happy evening of sometimes hilarity but always left us, at bedtime, with a warm feeling of togetherness and hope.

"TAKE COVER"
The Air-Raid
Siren goes off !
1942/3

THE GREAT
WAR
1914-18
"The War
and all
wars"

"TAKE COVER!"

The Air Raid Warning Siren stood on top of the Police Station in Windsor Road. When it sounded the "Alert" warning, its ear piercing insistent banshee wailing quickly cleared the streets of Penarth, as people scurried to whatever public air-raid shelters had been provided. A large brick built single storey windowless rectangular block stood in Albert Road in a yard beside the Old Post Office and many households had either an Anderson Shelter, half buried in the back garden or a table-like cage indoors.

Everyone would wait with baited breath during these air-raids, waiting for the whistling down of bombs and the "c-r-u-m-p", muffled sound of a distant explosion possibly bringing death, injury and destruction to Penarth. Although our town suffered a few deaths and some destruction, it was nothing like on the scale of that of Cardiff or Swansea.

But we were always fearful when that banshee wailing started up.

Gas masks had been issued to everyone and we were supposed to carry these with us everywhere, in their rigid plain cardboard boxes with the string halter. Even to school.

It happened only a few times during the schoolday. But then we would "take cover", huddling down underneath our desks listening for the drone of aeroplanes above and the rapid "pom-pom-pom" of the local ack-ack guns. Through the lozenge shaped spaces between the protective brown gummed paper on the windows, one might catch a glimpse of an air-raid warden, observing and watching to see if any incendiary bombs might have set fires alight in homes or shops and if so, send help.

At last the more leisurely slow wailing of the same siren sounded out the "All Clear" and we would get up, waiting for the teacher to do likewise and tell us what to do next.

Usually this instruction was to run home as fast as we could but "not to forget your gasmasks!"

We left school at a run, "just in case THEY came back", but ever curious to see what damage might have been done and to see if we could find any pieces of shrapnel, still hot, lying in the gutters.

It was war. But to us kids, it was strangely exciting and, only when one's own family suffered the consequences, did the true horror of its reality hit one.

"WALTER MITTY" MICKEY

"WALTER MITTY MICKEY"

It seems to me that I have always been cursed (or blessed) with an impulse to exaggerate or to fantasize. I could never be an historian or a journalist. It has become a standing joke with some of my friends, Martyn Howells in particular, that some of my long held misconceptions are really outrageously funny

One example, often repeated by grinning Martyn is that "Queen Victoria could speak no English until she was about forty! I blush quietly to myself at the memory of some of my other almost Mrs Malapropisms, although more factual than verbal convolutions. And maybe, if I ever get as far as to write "Confessions of a Retired Teacher", I will one day own up to some pretty absurd gems uttered to young impressionable schoolkids. I don't think they suffered too badly with me though. (Sorry, if any did fail to become respected journalists or historians because of my influence!)

My brother Jack tells me that in this respect though, I resemble another brother, George, who as a pre-war trainee travelling quantity surveyor with Western Trinidad Lake Asphalt Company, kept many pub audiences regaled with a flow of facts and figures, never challenged but made up spontaneously and convincingly to such effect. In later years, as an Advisory Teacher I recognised this quirk in human nature, i.e. "if in doubt, say it more loudly and irrefutably, and people will believe you". I was wary not to use this without some qualification but now realize it is one of the principal weapons in the armoury of some trades, notably those masters of the ploy: careerist politicians.

One of my earliest remembered "Walter Mitty"* Moments happened in Mr Roberts' class at breaktime. Morning break brought us all gathering to drink our small, third pint, bottle of milk and Milk Monitors were allowed to linger in the warmth of the classroom rather than go outside into the battleground of the cold playground. And here we would gather by the big wall radiator to yarn.

Kids, being kids, boasting of one's experiences and trying to "top" the last boaster's claims and so impress everyone, I remember claiming that I had once sailed on the famous liner, "The Queen Mary". This time however jeers of derision rather than the hoped for gasps of admiration, "Cor, Did yer?", greeted my claim.

Highly indignant at this aspersion on my honesty, I protested that my claim was true and that I had a photo of my Mam carrying me off the Queen Mary, when it stopped at Penarth Pier. At this they just howled for me to bring the evidence. Next day I took the clinching photo to school. Here it is reproduced. I am the "blondie" being carried by Mam, in her cloche hat.

Although the other kids pointed out that it must have been a Campbells' Paddle Steamer from which I disembarked at Penarth Pier, I still persisted in that belief that I had once sailed on the Queen Mary!

Come on! Own up! Haven't you ever had a "Walter Mitty" Moment ? (Politicians, excused)

---

* "Walter Mitty". A famous film (50s ?) with Danny Kaye, renowned American comic actor, playing the title role. This character had such flights of fantasy as being a stoic British Captain of a storm tossed sailing ship, battling with stiff upper-lip Englishness despite a broken arm; a tiger-fighting explorer in darkest Africa, etc, etc, whilst famously replying to his psychiatrist's question as to why he had never actually done any of these things in real life rather than the quiet timid life he had led: "My mother never let me cross the road!"

Horses.
Horse Shows
Gymkanas and
Horses. (1940-1970)

92

HORSES

From an early age, Pop would take me everywhere to see horses. This practice probably pre-dated my birth and certainly continued over decades with my nephew, Richard; later still with my own sons, Andrew and Seimon. From a then infant Royal Welsh Show to St Mary Hill Fair, near Bridgend, where we would watch the gypsies, or didicais, examining their potential new purchase's yellowing teeth and trotting various ponies across the rough grassy hillside with a mate carefully observing the animal's gait – to the upmarket "Wenvoe Horseshow" where wealthy and immaculately clad ladies and gentlemen politely clapped famous equestrian Colonel Harry Llewellyn on his fine mount "Foxhunter", as he cleared yet another perfect round of the gates.

But the highlight of the year was always the annual pilgrimage to Bridgewater Fair in Somerset, later to become a spectacular three day event with parades of illuminated floats, jazz bands, fairgrounds and pop music. At that time however, it still had all the atmosphere of a medieval country fair, where again horses were bought and sold as well as local produce.

At that time also, the mass production of mushrooms had not yet appeared and Pop would always make a point of buying as many baskets of freshly harvested mushrooms as we could carry home with us and, later still, would still make a nuisance of himself trying to sell them and even, at ninety, pestering the waiting customers in the Old Post Office.

My enthusiasm for this pilgrimage, and that of the later generations of children, eventually waned with the reluctance to get up at 4.30 a.m. to walk down to Cogan to get either a hired coach or train and henceforth Pop would go alone. Later we would always regret having not gone with him-no more so than on the final occasion when he failed to return and the Bridgewater Police found him asleep and confused on the station platform the following day.

These childhood memories would be incomplete without this recollection of horses and their importance to Pop and another strand of our shared experiences.

"American" Balloons? 1945

94

"AMERICAN BALLOONS" ???

(Penarth – 1944/45)

The "Ragged-Arsed-Rovers" of The Triangle Gang were at large again. (Thank G., no ASBOS then, otherwise all my friends... and me too, little Mickey Drippin', would have earned a full set or more by now!)

Penarth was strangely quiet. The Americans had left behind their Nissen Huts in O'Neale's Wood (now Northcliffe Estate - next to present-day "Headlands school").

We had not realized the significance of all those flat-bottomed barges, with the odd drop-down hinged metal doors, which had previously lain forlornly about on the shingle beach near Penarth Docks. Now they had disappeared too.

So, bored and with time hanging, as usual, we wandered through the woods, climbing trees, tearing our pants, shouting and whooping as only real Red Indians could, "cowboys or "windy-bums"- all. Some, hungry kids, as always, tried tasting the beech-mast, declaring it: "smashin'", but surreptitiously spitting it out and grinning if we had caught out someone else, stupid enough to believe us.

Then a few of us idly inspected the outside of one of the empty Nissen Huts. One lad even got upon his pal's back to stare through into the hut, cupping his hands round his eyes to see more clearly the dark interior. "Cor! Comics!", he yelped as he fell back.

That was enough for all of us. With the help of a rusty penknife the sort of soft bakelite window was carved open and we got inside.

The jumbled mess of this Marie Celeste mysterious scene of abandonment tempted us to explore further. Away in one seemingly empty locker, on the floor lay a small pile of tiny packets. Ripping one open, I found curious balloons-all the same creamy whitish colour. The other kids hadn't noticed me rummaging around, I suppose. They were all too absorbed in finding comics or a few odd broken packs of "Camel" cigarettes.

Laying on the empty bunks, one or two were even pretending to be GIs, reading their "funnies" and smoking/coughing away at a Camel.

I stuffed a few of the packets in my pocket and, only later on the way home – finding a bit of string amongst the other junk in my bulging pockets, blew up the first "balloon" I had freed from its packet, tied the length of string to it and, trailing it behind me, went down the front steps under the archway and through the door opposite the "coal shed".... and in.

Mam smiled as I went into the basement sitting room. "Look what I've got!" I proudly called. But, puzzling this, she didn't seem at all pleased at my find of American Balloons. In fact, she took them all away, before sending me to the shops. But I could have sworn I saw a funny little smile on her face... though she was a bit red.... must have been that old fire... no need on a sunny day like that!

20 [...] (82.) Victory Party and The Nazi Flag.

THE VICTORY STREET PARTY AND THE NAZI PAPER FLAG
Penarth – St Augustine's Road – 1945

Everything was ready!

All the Mams had helped set out the tables in the street for our Victory Party and laden them with Jellies, cakes, sandwiches and everything they could get hold of to make our party the best street party in town. So we sat down out in the road, just by the Triangle and near my best pal, Arthur's house. We sat near the end of the table, with Arthur just to my right, at the end of our row, Brian Baynham at the head of the table and Dennis Mayne sitting in a deck chair , by his side. . Several of Arthur's Aunties stood on one side of the table, one of them holding up Young Bob, Arthur's brother. He had on a paper hat miles too big for him, which just about covered his face ! Someone took a photo of us all.

Then just as the party was coming to an end, Pop came up, holding his wrist and asking if I knew where Mam was. He had slipped on the "Red Path": usual way down to John Street and Nellie's, the corner shop there. Then he went off to get some help for himself.

As evening drew on, we all got ready for the next big event:- the bonfire just up a small rise above us in The Triangle. Some people had made an effigy of Adolf Hitler to burn on the bonfire. It was then that I remembered the old paper Nazi flag.-sort of triangular shape and with an enormous black swastika. But someone had spoilt it by writing all over it in ink. It was funny old writing. Although I was a good reader in school, I couldn't understand any of it. It must have been in German, I suppose. Anyway I ran to get it out of the old wardrobe on the top landing, where it had lain for years, probably from before the war *.

Later, how we all cheered when the flames from the bonfire caught old Adolf and he and the paper flag flared up and burnt away. "Good Riddance to bad rubbish! "a number of the older people were all saying as tired out but really happy, we went off home to bed.

Yeah, our street party had been THE BEST IN ALL OF PENARTH, we all agreed.

---

*A few years later**, my brother Jack told me the history of the Nazi Paper pennant. Before the war, a party of young Austrians had arrived in the town, looking for somewhere to camp. Local Organisers of this annual visit had arranged for them to use the site of the old (WW1) gun emplacements near the former Artillery House (now demolished but part of the site of Uppercliffe Estate near Penarth Head.) It was only a few days later that one of the Austrian party was taking photos of this very same Pennant, which had been hoisted to the top of the old flag pole which still stood there. This Pennant had been left behind and was evidently the very same one which was ultimately burned on the St Augustine's Road Victory Party bonfire. Appropriately it was last seen burning around the neck of Hitler's effigy, also consumed by the flames! **Years later again**, while studying German, I came to regret that this artefact of the era was ,lost for ever, without those Nazi sentiments ever having been recorded! **(See also the 1934 - Autumn edition * of "The Penarthian" (County School mag) for an interesting article by one student, returned from a trip to Germany: his enthusiasm for the Nazi regime and belief in the peaceable intentions of the Nazi Party was quite common in Britain at the time. (*My brother, Jack, still has one)).**

Mickey (The mouse) 1910#7.
and "THE MAN IN BLACK" 82.

7.3.07

98

MICKEY (THE MOUSE) AND THE MAN IN BLACK

1946/47? ...aged about 12 or 13 or even later.

'The Man in Black" was a very popular radio drama series, as far as I can recollect just after The War. It was narrated by Valentine Dyall - an actor with a deep echoing rich and most atmospheric voice, which lent great gravitas to the half-hour story he related each Friday evening, finishing precisely at 9 p.m. with the sound of Big Ben's Chimes just before the BBC News. The story itself may well have been acted out, but it was his voice-over which gave most of the sinister hair-raising, Edgar Alan Poe-ish quality to the tales of horror and terror Valentine Dyall related, with such effect.

It was compulsive listening in those days, prior to the banale street wisdom and unphaze-ability of to day's Chain Saw Massacre afficionados. But the word pictures summoned up in those post-war days, when one would have thought that the General Public, after six long years of Total war with all its atrocities, should have been sickened by or at least inured to yet more horror. But 'The Man in Black' drew huge audiences to their wireless sets to be frightened and then, at Nine O'clock, relieved to be released from their terror by the BBC News, whatever world disaster or calamity was reported upon, seemed unreal and fairly mild in contrast to the previous drama.

One such Friday evening, I, Mickey Ford, settled down on my own in the basement sitting room of home: No 26, Pembroke Terrace, Penarth, to listen again to The Man in Black. I was on my own in the house as Mam had, for once gone to the local cinema, the Washington with my sisters. It may have been a Charles Boyer film as he was Mam's innocent "heart-throb" and though she didn't go often to the cinema this must have been quite an occasion for her.

The room was lit only by gaslight and the flickering glow of the fire from the old Welsh Fire-range and the darkness of the outside winter evening was even more intensified by the overshadowing street above and the outside stone steps which led down from it.

As the story line became more and more terrifying, I too became ever more conscious of my own vulnerability in that room, all alone at home in the old, old house. Carefully I took appropriate precautions, grabbing the long solid iron poker from the hearth and burying myself in the depths of the corner armchair, I turned up the gas light as high as possible.

From the wireless the lugubrious voice, relentlessly, with appropriate sound effects, drove the incredible story of the mad scientist on and on and the tension rose and rose as the hands of the mantelpiece clock moved ever closer to nine 0' clock and the hour at which the madman was going to perform the hideously grotesque operation of brain-removal, without anaesthetic- of course - upon his already screaming victim. Rescuers were, of course / racing to the scene to prevent the evil deed but inevitably delayed by the London Traffic and the fog-induced accidents, it was literally a race against death ... .and at the first stroke of Big Ben over the air waves the programme ended abruptly but suggestively also with a prolonged scream.

By this time I had dashed to the door to the basement courtyard and, with poker still in my hand, scrambled up to the deserted street of Pembroke Terrace -lit only by a gas street lamp on the comer. There I remained, waiting for Mam and my sisters to return from the cinema, but at least had the presence of mind to hide the poker as they approached and mumbled sheepishly some excuse for being out on the road alone. They must have wondered why all the doors of the house were open and the inside gas lights turned up high.

I don't think I ever did listen to the wireless again on a Friday evening at half-past-eight!

FIRST ART LESSON
AT THE GRAMMAR SCHOOL
PRIMARY COLOURS and SECONDARY?.
September 1945

STUPID BOY!??
10·3·07

PRIMARY COLOURS AND SECONDARY

I had passed the scholarship examination and here I was in Form 1A at Penarth County Grammar School, eager eyed and bushy tailed, raring to go. Four others from Albert Road Elementary School had passed also and were in the same class, Peter Adams, Peter Frost, Stan Jones and "Nobby" Clarke. I sat beside George Best.* No, not the footballer but son of a sometime visitor to us at No 26, owner of a smallholding in Sully.

But things had not started very auspiciously. The Form House Captains had been chosen by popular acclaim by the class and they in turn picked out their teams for the School Houses of Archer, Stanwell, Plymouth and Windsor. The most popular boys and conspicuously self-confident and sporty were picked early and I remained unpicked amongst those few unpicked still seated. I was not quite last and ended up in the least popular House. A good start!

I could write a fair story even then and was quite proud of this until the lady English Teacher started correcting my grammar and speech. How was I to know that it was "wrong" for me to write "pub"when it was slang for "public house"? And the usual Penarthism "going down the beach." and other colloquialisms were also not to be tolerated. The brightness of eye and the bushiness of my tail began to weaken a fraction.

But worse was to come with the first Art Lesson. From day one, the teacher and I seemed to take a mutual dislike for each other. At the very start of this first lesson he quizzed me, "What are the Primary Colours and what are the Secondary Colours?". I had to confess that I just did not know. Then followed the first of the many occasions with him that I was ordered as "a stupid boy" to stand on the desk for the remainder of the lesson, which lasted about 40 minutes. I came to dread art and loathe school. It was little wonder that from Form 1A, for the rest of my schooldays at the County School, I moved through all the "B" forms.

Later that term, my eldest brother visited the school to enquire about my lack of progress and changed attitude to school, having already become aware of my terror on "Art Days" and it was explained that the particular teacher with the sadistic streak had been a victim of the first world war and as a result of his severe injuries had great personal health and mood problems.

I often make a joke of my namesake ancestor (unproven) who developed automation in the American Car Industry, and that my aversion to using colour is because of his famous saying about his Model Ts, "Any colour you like, as long as it's black !" but probably you'll agree that my early introduction to Primary and Secondary Colours was just a bit unfortunate.

* George, also a now-retired teacher, is well known in the town as compiler/author of the annual "Penarth Calendar" – with its selected postcard scenes of old Penarth.

Preparation Hardening Up!

Hey You! Mickey Drippin'! WANNA FIGHT?

Mickey giving his "executioner" a lift to the fight!

"The Big Fight" Pembroke Terrace, Penarth; September 1945

82.

THE BIG FIGHT

In my home, one never heard voices raised in anger. Pop and Mam were gentle folk. Despite hardship and setbacks, there had never been a time of violence or force. As I have already described I lived a quiet relatively happy life without confrontation and surrounded mostly by women and girls.

But one day as I was collecting my bike from the school bike sheds, I heard from behind me the mocking call, "Hey you, Mickey Drippin', Wanna Fight?"

So when I heard this challenge just a short time into my first term at the County School, I was overwhelmed, confused, distraught. But even then, I could hardly show myself to be a coward. So I accepted, even though with a heavy heart. The two kids from my form were obviously enjoying my visible discomfort and grinning like the proverbial Cheshire Cats. But for me, with no experience of fisticuffs, it was no joke. Quite out of my depth, I even awkwardly offered my challenger a lift home on the crossbar of my bike and he, still grinning and winking at his mate running alongside, accepted and so we, or rather I toiled up Albert Road Hill, past our old school and into Pembroke Terrace. There next to the Sea Cadet Hut was a square concrete base for a hut which had stood there amongst the long rough grass. This was to be our boxing ring. For some reason, The Big Fight was arranged for later that same day. While the two laughing lads went home for a while, I climbed the bank and within a few yards reached my house. No one at home. How does one fight ? I asked myself. "Important to be tough". "To have hard fists!", I decided. So with no-one else at home I tried to toughen myself up...without any real idea of how this could be achieved in the short space of time before "my execution".

You'll probably have guessed that I was not over-confident of the outcome of my first ever fight.

"Harden your fists !" I had decided so set about hitting mine against the wooden drawers of the sideboard and although wincing with the unaccustomed pain hoped that this would do the trick.

Punctually at the appointed hour I appeared at "The Ring". As did the two jokers.

After a few wild swings of my flailing arms, the two simply collapsed with laughter and my ordeal was over.

"Better to have fought and lost than never to have fought at all", I thought. But maybe that was wrong. I had survived though! Just for now.

VIPVisit to my class (1A) at Penarth County School

October 1945

V.I.P. VISITOR TO FORM 1A

The lesson had started in our classroom when there came a tap on the door and the Headmaster came in.

"We have a visitor today, Form 1A", he announced. "He was a pupil at this school before the war and he is now a pilot in the R.A.F." The Head seemed to be smiling in my direction but even so, I didn't guess who this V.I.P visitor might be. The other boys looked up with rapt attention.

To my delight and great pride, in walked my brother George, resplendent in his uniform complete with pilot's wings. Our teacher, one of the older ones in the school, instantly smiled and went forward to shake George's hand. George winked at me and the teacher explained that this was my brother and that he had indeed taught George before the war.

I glowed with pride and could hardly contain myself at the new stares of wonderment and almost respect from my curious classmates. They seemed almost astounded that this former "reject" from the House Choosing session could have such an obviously heroic brother as George.

For a few weeks, I was able to enjoy and almost bask in George's reflected glory, but sadly a terrible event was to follow.

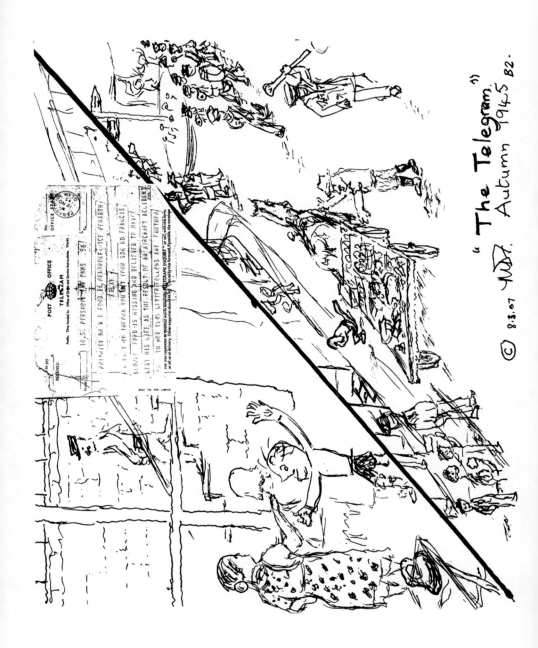

"The Telegram." Autumn 1945 B2.

© 8.3.07 M.D.F.

THE TELEGRAM

It was Saturday, November 10th 1945. Saturday was always the busiest and most important day of the week for the Ford family of Pembroke Terrace, Penarth. It could be said that our very survival depended on the trading success of Saturday as this was the day of "The Round", when Dad (a.k.a. "Pop"), having collected the produce from his smallholding near the Toll Gate on Penarth Road, more fruit and Veg from the warren of wholesalers around Custom House Street , Cardiff and breakfasted for the last time at about 9.30 a.m. would load up the cart with the last essentials from the basement scullery and prepare to leave on the day-long "round" of his customers around the streets of Penarth. I, his youngest son —then aged 11, had taken up the outside stone steps the scales and the weights:14lb,7, 4, 2, 1 a half pound, quarter and two ounces with which I knew all combinations were possible. Pop was carrying out a last minute check to see that everything was loaded.

Then, waiting with Mam and sister Bea, we caught sight of the telegram-boy coming down the steps from the street above.

Knowing that my RAF pilot brother George was already engaged to a W.A.A.F. (member of the Women's Air force) and that a baby was expected, I let out a whoop, guessing (wrongly) that it was to announce their hasty wedding. But Mam had already guessed the real purpose of the telegram now being brought to our downstairs door by a very sober looking telegram boy.

Supported and comforted by my sister Bea, just 9 years older than myself, mam sank quietly sobbing onto the battered old couch. I was equally shattered by the news that George "was missing believed to have lost his life", just the previous day. But before anything more could be said, mam turned to me and begged me not to tell Pop. It was vital that The Round be got through. I, as usual, was to go with him but not breathe a word about the telegram. Pop would be told the terrible news at the end of the day.

That day is a memory that still haunts me, although I know that countless thousands of other families suffered the same traumatic period. But for an eleven year old boy to keep such a terrible secret from his dear father for a whole day, serving customers, hiding the welling tears, trying to smile at any jokes between Pop and the customers was the most difficult task of my life.

All went reasonably well until late afternoon, when approaching Penarth Centre Roundabout, the sounds of martial music, a whole band and an approaching parade, became louder and louder. Then, confronting us came the parade, headed by an airman with pilot's wings who seemed to me the spitting image of my now dead brother. To my father's puzzlement, I could hold out no longer, and with a howl of anguish fled through the nearby Windsor Arcade, closely followed by my mongrel dog, Bulla.

It had, I now presume, been The Armistice Day Parade but to me such occasions are just too poignant to celebrate or even watch with a feeling other than one of horror.

Pop would learn later and grieve but The Round and The Day had been saved and Pop spared for just a few more hours.

Grief
and
Christmas

"GRIEF AND CHRISTMAS"

Brother George, an RAF Pilot, had been killed in an aircraft accident on 9th November.

Now with Christmas approaching, a large well wrapped box arrived through the post, addressed to me! At eleven years, despite the cloud of grief hanging over us all at home, I was excited to find out what this unexpected parcel contained and sister Bea helped me unwrap it, whilst Mam looked on.

To Bea's horror and Mam's tears, a carefully handcrafted model aeroplane was revealed, a black painted replica of the type of large bomber in which our Dear George, then aged only 24, had lost his life only weeks before. No cruel joke this but a quite innocently intended Christmas gift from Uncle Frank in High Wycombe, but unfortunately much delayed in the post.

To my then childish feeble protests, Mam picked up the black winged model and quietly sobbing dropped it into the midst of the fiery coals of the old Welsh fire range where it was slowly consumed by the flames and dissolved into curling black embers. Quietly Bea and I watched and seeing Mam's grief bowed back, still quivering, I quietened and vaguely understood why such a present at such a time just had to end in the way it did.

****

But the approach of Christmas was still undeniable. And I was the youngest child. Nine years separated me from the next youngest, sister Bea. Mam had by now lost four of her original eight children, with her (and our) latest tragic loss so very recent and understandably potentially destructive of our family morale.

Only much later in adulthood, did I fully understand what Mam's ordeal that Christmas must have been for her and how she, and Pop, but mainly Mam with that heroic understanding and self sacrifice ever displayed by mothers everywhere, managed to set aside her grief or rather to prioritise the urgent childlike needs of immature me, eleven years old and desperately still wanting to experience the customary child's "Christmas in Wales".

"Do you really want us to celebrate Christmas this year, Mickey ?" she quietly asked.

Of course, my answer meant that "the decorations went up", the magical appearance of the morning stocking — stuffed with maybe a few small toys but mostly nuts, sweets, an apple and even a gaily wrapped tangerine bringing squeals of delight at its discovery on Christmas morn with the merrily tuneful carillon of St Augustines' bells vigorously rung by old Mr Dorman throughout the morning and the sights, sounds and mouth-watering smells of our festive Christmas family dinner being prepared by Mam and Bea, while brother Jack and Pop played with me.

What it must have cost the rest of the family in hidden emotions and all for my sake!

But their hidden pains assured me of a sense of normality and stability, which I remember to this day and count as an immense gift, the most precious any family could bestow on any child at Christmastime.

THE ROAD TO RECOVERY/A NEW MENTOR.

2007   B2.

110

THE ROAD TO RECOVERY AND A NEW MENTOR

As soon as the tragic news had arrived that brother George was "missing, believed to have lost his life", brother Jack was immediately granted compassionate leave and came home, and using George's old car started visiting RAF camps, such as Stormy Down to try to get more news. George's plane had gone down into the Bristol Channel off Porthcawl but, despite nearby ships having searched for many hours, only one crewman was ever found. Neither George nor any of the other crewmembers were ever found and now the family had to grieve but hope at some stage to start to recover from this tragedy.

Mam had now lost four of her original eight children and I had only one surviving brother.

Over the years I came to realize that for Jack, besides his own grief over the loss of a beloved brother, only four years separating them both, he had to get used to me, the spoilt brat sixteen years his junior. We were almost strangers to each other and it took some adjusting for us both.

But Jack set about supporting Mam and Pop, improving their living conditions and also their lives by taking us out in the car which he had inherited from George. Unused to having a car, this became an eye-opener for us all in turn. Our Sunday outings became a firm favourite and together we explored the countryside. Even before Dyffryn Gardens were open to the public we visited there. Even Pop enjoyed for the first time in his life a visit to Cowbridge on Boxing Day to follow the traditional Hunt.

Gradually Jack also became a great friend and mentor, taking a great interest in me and my wider education. With another ex-serviceman, Lynn Williams, of Lime Kiln Cottage, in a field off Penarth Road, he would drive us both up to near the Cliff Walk, where, with Autumn mists swirling around us outside, we would read aloud The Pickwick Papers and laugh at the antics and verbosity of Mr Pickwick, Mr Jingle, Sam Weller and all the other myriad of Dickens characters.

As time went by he introduced me to theatre going and Shaw, as well as seeing in The Prince of Wales Theatre, Cardiff, one of the last of the great actor-managers, Donald Wolfitt playing King Lear and melodramatically hanging on to the curtain at the end, booming, "friends.....", whilst theatrically mopping his brow. Teaching me to swim at my age of thirteen, film-going together to the Globe cinema in Cardiff to watch Fernandel, the famous French comic, all these experiences were yet to come, but Jack was an essential leader on the slow road to recovery.

And it is to Jack that I owe so much for any successes which I later achieved and came to understand those lines from Kipling's "If":

("If you can meet with) triumph and disaster, and treat those two imposters both the same!"

Pop had been a stalwart and loving father, who had given me such a secure base to build on. Now Jack, old enough to be another father to me, became the necessary guide into a rich world of the mind.

"On the Home Front", Mam and Pop had surpassed themselves in their nurturing of me. Now, with such a wise new additional mentor, the future beckoned with even more promise.

"Pop" with one of his adored grandchildren,
Judith, daughter of author's brother, Jack.
Probably taken about 1956

No. 26 (now No. 12), Pembroke Terrace home of the Ford family for over 60 years, is the second from the right

Mike Ford

The author was born at home, as were his seven siblings, in the house shown above. Now aged 73, he has spent nearly his whole life resident in the town and started writing and illustrating these stories for his seven grandchildren.

This book: "On the home front" gives his impressions of life in and around his home from 1934 until 1946. It is the second book in the intended series, "PENARTH... Not the Centre of the Universe, BUT..." The first book, "Albert Road Boys First" dealt with his (mis)adventures in and around the elementary school he attended between 1938 and 1945.

It is hoped to continue the series with further books of reminiscences following his life and times.